MACHINE LANGUAGE

PROGRAMMING

MADE SIMPLE FOR YOUR

SINCLAIR ZX 80 & ZX 81

First Published in the United Kingdom
by Melbourne House

This Remastered Edition
Published in 2022 by
Acorn Books
acornbooks.uk

This book is a page-by-page reproduction of the original 1981 edition as published by Melbourne House. The entirety of the book is presented with no changes, corrections nor updates to the original text, images and layout; therefore no guarantee is offered as to the accuracy of the information within.

INDEX

FINDING YOUR WAY

AROUND

MACHINE LANGUAGE

<u>THE BEGINNING:</u>

This book is designed to be an introduction the field of machine and assembly language programming for the Sinclair ZX80 and ZX81.

It may be that you are coming to this book with no clear idea of what machine language programming is all about. Indeed the difference between machine language and assembly language may not be clear to you, nor indeed how they differ from programming in BASIC.

So let us look at the way a computer operates:

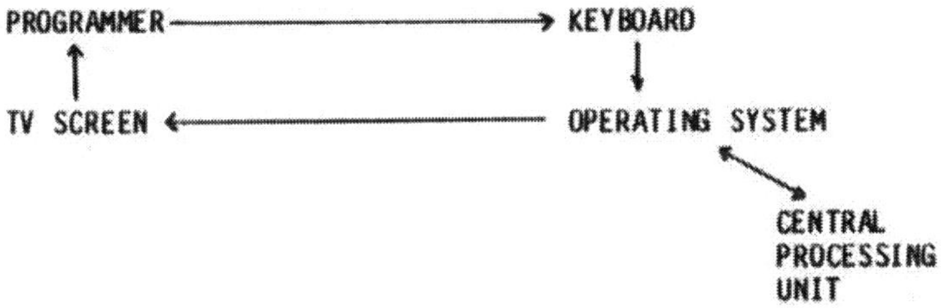

What this diagram shows is that there is a barrier between the programmer and the central proccessing unit of the computer. It is not possible under normal programming for the programmer to tell the central processing unit - usually referred to as the <u>CPU</u> - what to do.

In the Sinclair machines the CPU is a Z80A chip, and I am sure it comes as no surprise to learn that the Z80A does not understand a word of "BASIC"!

<u>Indeed no CPU is able to be programmed in a way that is directly readable by humans.</u>

If you think about it for long enough, you will realise that it would be impossible in any case to give a chip in a computer an instruction that would make any sense to a human. Take the top off your Sinclair and have a look at the chip marked ˝NEC˝ - this is the Z80A CPU. Obviously this chip in your computer can only respond to electrical signals that are passed on to it by the rest of the circuitry!

The way this chip is designed, it can accept signals simultaneously from eight of the pins connected to it.
Keeping in mind that what is really happening is electrical signals, we can still adopt a convention to represent these signals - for example showing a ˝1˝ if there is a signal, or a ˝0˝ if there is no signal.

A typical instruction might therefore look something like:

    0 0 1 1 1 1 0 0

Quite a long way from something like

    ˝Let A = A + 1˝,

for example, isn˝t it!

Nonetheless, this is what machine language is all about. The name says it all! It is a language for machines.

At this stage you may be asking yourself - if this is what machine language programming is all about, why bother? Why not accept the benefits of someone else˝s work which allows us to program the computer in a language we can all understand, such as Basic or Cobol?

The Main Benefits Of Machine Language Are:

FASTER EXECUTION OF THE PROGRAM

MORE EFFICIENT USE OF MEMORY

SHORTER PROGRAMS (IN MEMORY)

FREEDOM FROM OPERATING SYSTEM

All of the above benefits are a direct result of programming in a language that the CPU can understand without having to have it translated first.

When you program in Basic, the operating system is the program that is really being run by the machine. The program is something like:

```
NEXT    Look at next instruction
        Translate it into machine language
        Perform that instruction
        Store the result if required
        Go to NEXT again
```

This method of programming is up to 60 times slower than a program written directly in machine language!

Nonetheless, we would have to be among the first to admit that programming in machine language does have some drawbacks.

THE MAIN DISADVANTAGES OF MACHINE LANGUAGE ARE:

PROGRAMS DIFFICULT TO READ AND DEBUG

IMPOSSIBLE TO ADAPT TO OTHER COMPUTERS

LONGER PROGRAMS (IN INSTRUCTIONS)

ARITHMETIC CALCULATIONS DIFFICULT

This means that we must make a very conscious decision of which programming method we should use for particular applications.
A very long program for financial applications should be written in a language designed to deal with numbers and one in which programs can be easily modified if required.

On the other hand there is nothing quite so bad as an arcade game written in basic - when you get down to it, it is just too slow.

Your own needs, the amount of memory in your computer, the time to put into programming, and so on will determine your choice of programming language.

MACHINE VS. ASSEMBLY LANGUAGE:

There is only one major difference between assembly language and machine language: assembly language is more easily read by humans than machine language (but on the other hand, computers can't read assembly language).

Assembly language is a partial translation of machine language so that it can be read by humans in a form that is easier to understand than
0 1 1 1 0 1 1 1.

It is not an adaptation of machine language, such as BASIC. In assembly language there is one and only one instruction for each machine language instruction (and there is only one machine language instruction for each asssembly language instruction).

We therefore say that assembly language is <u>equivalent</u> to machine language.

Assembly language makes use of Mnemomics (or abbreviations). For example at this stage, the instruction

```
INC   HL
```

may not mean much to you, but at least you can read it. It you were told that "INC" is a standard abbreviation (or mnemonic) for increase and that HL is a variable, then by simply looking at that instruction you can get a feel for what is happening.

The same instruction in machine language is

```
23
```

Now obviously you can also "read" that instruction, in the sense that you can read the number, but it isn't going to mean much to you unless you have a table to look up.

Assembly language can be converted directly to machine code by a program or by you. The program is called an assembler, and we understand that an assembler for the ZX 81 is soon to be available.

Nonetheless, such assemblers typically require 6K of memory, and this is not going to be much use if you have only 1 - 4 K of memory.

You will have to do the translation of mnemonics by hand, using the tables provided in this book.

It's hard, it's frustrating, it's inconvenient, but it's wonderful practice and gives you a great insight into the way computers work.

CPU
7
5
3
1
9
2
11

WHAT IS THE CPU

If we want to talk the same language as the CPU we have to know what sort of a person the CPU is. Eventually you may be asking the CPU to do some quite remarkable tasks from playing chess to keeping your books of accounts.

The CPU is no big mystery. I like to think of the CPU as a lonely little fellow, sitting in the middle of your Sinclair, being asked to do things all the time.

Especially calculations.

But the poor fellow doesn't even have a piece of paper and pencil to keep track of what is happening. How does he do it?

Let us look at one example in more detail - say you want the CPU to work out the time in New York, knowing the time in London.

Now given that the CPU doesn't know anything, first of all you tell it what the time in London is: 10 o'clock. The CPU has nowhere to keep this information and doesn't know what you will ask it to do next, so it puts that information away in a box, say box #1.

Then you tell it the time difference, say five hours earlier, and it puts that away in box #2.

Comes the time for calculations, it races across to box #1, gets the number, goes to box #2, performs the calculation, and puts the result away, say in box #3.

$$10 - 5 = 5$$

The answer of course is 5 O clock.

All of this racing between boxes, adding, subtracting and so on would be extremely tedious if the CPU had to do it all in its head, so it does exactly what you or I would do - it counts on its fingers and toes.

The CPU's hands and feet are called Registers

The Z80 chip is remarkable among CPU's in that it has a lot of hands and toes - but we will get to that later.

In our time difference analysis above, we actually skipped a step when we just glibly said "performs the calculation".

The example is one you might be able to do in your head, but if you were given two large numbers to add without the benefit of calculator or pencil and paper you might have some difficulty. So let's go back to our time difference example:

For simplicity's sake, let's call one of the CPU's hands "Hand A". How does the CPU manipulate the contents of the box #1 and box #2? The following sequence is pretty close to what the CPU would actually do

* Count out the value of box #1 on the fingers of Hand A;

* Subtract the contents of box #2 from what he has already on his fingers;

* Look at the value on the fingers of Hand A and store it in box #3.

Now if this is what truly happens, there are some pretty phenomenal conclusions to be drawn from this:

1. The CPU would not be able to deal with a number like 11.53 - it could only deal in whole numbers.

2. The CPU would be limited in its calculations to whatever number it could count to on its fingers.

This is true!

The main consolation however is that the CPU has a lot of hands and feet and can keep count on each of them separately, and that it can count to 255 using only the 8 fingers of Hand A.

We will deal in the next chapter with the details of how the CPU can count up to more than 8 on each hand while we can only manage 10 using two hands! Suffice it to say that each hand can count to 255 and each foot can be used to count to over 64,000!

The time difference execise above has still not been represented in anything like the language the CPU understands - all we have done is describe the processes. Let us now use mnemonics (Abbreviations) to instruct the CPU at each step:

```
SETTING UP:
        LD (BOX #1),  10
        LD (BOX #2),  5
CALCULATING:
        LD A, (BOX #1)
        SUB A, (BOX #2)
        LD (BOX #3), A
```

These instructions may seem a little terse at first, but after all menmonics are mnemonics. "LD is an abbreviation for "load" so that

LD A,1

for example, would mean load A with 1 : that is count off 'one' on the fingers of hand A.

We also use a rather clever image in these menmonics by the use of brackets: the brackets are used to indicate we wish to deal with the contents of whatever is inside the brackets.

It should be fairly easy to remember this on a visual basis because brackets do look like they are meant to indicate a container.

So running through the mnemonics above, we load the contents of Box #1 and #2 with 10 and 5, ...etc... to get the final result of 5 in box #3.

All of this is fairly simple to follow and I am sure you can understand that while you are doing this calculation the numbers on hand "A" represent the time in New York. A minute later they may be used to represent the number of employees in a company, and at some other time how much money you have.

You may be used to the concept of variables from your BASIC programming, but this is a concept you must leave behind in machine language programming.

The fingers of Hand "A" are not a variable in the same sense as in a BASIC program. They are merely what the CPU uses to count with.

<u>One of the big differences in programming in machine language and</u>

<u>programming in Basic is in fact this lack of variables.</u>

It is always possible to store things away in the memory locations, or boxes as we called them in the above example. But these are not really variables either. They are however immensely useful, but no more than memory locations set aside for specific purposes.

Let us go back to the CPU and consider what happens if someone comes in to the room in the middle of a calculation? Embarrassing situation with fingers flying, all full of information that he can't afford to lose.

The polite thing to do would be to get up and shake hands, but what would happen to all those numbers? One solution would be to quickly write down all the numbers and store them in boxes. But then you would have to remember in which boxes you had stored the information - and where are you going to store the number that tells you where the information is?

Our CPU gets away with it by using one of those tall spiky things that some people keep bills, spare notes, etc. I am sure you know those stacks where you spike one piece of paper on and then the next, and so one. It's great if you want the top piece of paper only, but very inconvenient if you want to see what's in the middle because you have to go through all the pieces stuck on the spike.

This little stack, however, is ideally suited to our CPU because it only wants to look at the top piece of paper. When the "interrupt" comes, he puts all the information on the stack, and as soon as the interrupt is over, the CPU pops the top piece of paper off and continues with its calculation.

In computer terminology we call this spike a "STACK". When we put a piece of information of the stack we "PUSH" it on, and when we retrieve the information, we "POP" it off.

All kinds of information can be "PUSH"ed and "POP"ed on and off the stack - for example if the CPU was in the middle of a complex calculation when the interrupt came, not only would it need to save whatever information it had on its fingers and toes but also what point of the calculation he had reached. This would involve many separate "PUSH"es and then many separate "POP"s at the end.

The stack is also extremely useful if the CPU runs out of hands.

For reasons best known to itself our CPU likes to keep the stack stuck to the ceiling just above where he is working. This means that the more information is "PUSH"ed on, the further the stack grows downwards.

The main advantage of the stack is that the CPU does not need to remember which box the information is in - it knows it is the last piece "PUSH"ed on the stack, because it has organised itself so that it would always be so.

CPU

<u>THE WAY COMPUTERS COUNT</u>

We mentioned in the previous chaper that the CPU was able to count to 255 using only eight fingers. How can this be when with 10 fingers we can only manage to count to 10?

It is certainly not because computers are smarter (they aren´t) but because the CPU is more organised in its information than we are: why should raising your index finger have the same value (= ´1´) as having your little finger raised?

It seems obvious that if you so wished you could represent two different numbers in this way.

It is very much the same sort of thing as realising that the number 001 is different from the number 100. The plain truth is that humans are not very efficient in the use of fingers for counting.

The CPU understands that not having a finger is of some information and that which finger is raised is a valuable piece of information.

With only two fingers it ids possible to devise a way to count from 0 to 3, as follows:

00 = 0	We can indicate not having a finger raised as ´0´,
01 = 1	and having a finger raised as ´1´.
10 = 2	this does not mean 11 = 3.
11 = 3	It means we chose to let the representation 11 (or two fingers) have the value 3.

We could just as easily have chosen a different representation.

There is a direct relationship between this and binary representation. The CPU´s fingers are locations in memory and they can be made to indicate on and off (or ´0´ and ´1´ as convention dictates).

If we added a third finger to our example above we could represent all the numbers from 0 to 7. Three fingers for 0 - 7 !
Four fingers would be able to represent all the numbers from 0 to 15!

In order to simplify the notation of such numbers, and to avoid confusion in trying to write down the number eleven as opposed to indicating that two bits were set, a universal convention has been adopted:

The numbers 10 - 15 are indicated by the letters A - F.

Decimal	10	=>	A	(We show => as ´equal´)
	11	=>	B	
	12	=>	C	
	13	=>	D	
	14	=>	E	
	15	=>	F	

Simple isn´t it?

This way of treating numbers is called the Hexadecimal Format.

In machine language programming, it is . convenient to deal with numbers in a Hexadecimal Format.

This is only a convention and if you so wished you could write all your instruction in normal decimal format. Naturally you would need a program to convert the decimal notation to binary bits being on and off. But this is not a major problem because we use a program to convert the hexadecimal notation to binary bits.

It is convenient for us to use the hexadecimal format because:

1. It is easy to convert from this form to binary,which tells us which bit (or finger) is doing what.

2. It gives us an easy means of seeing whether numbers are 8-bit or 16-bit.

3. It standardises all numbers to sets of 2-digit numbers.

4. It is the common convention and familiarity with hexadecimal will allow you to read other books and manuals more easily.

But it is only a convention and not a sacred rule.

The hexadecimal system as we mentioned earlier, lets us represent the numbers 0 to 15 using only 4 bits. Any 8-bit memory location or 8-bit register can therefore be described by two sets of 4 bits.

(This is the same as saying that any combination of 10 fingers can be represented by two hands of 5 fingers each).

The reason we are concerned with 8-bit memory locations and 8-bit registers is that this is the structure of the Sinclair Computers. All memory locations and all single registers have 8 bits.

(This is not hard to conceptualise - it's like saying all humans have 5 fingers on each hand).

Taking things one step at a time, let us become familiar with 4 fingers first:

1 1 1 1 = 8 + 4 + 2 + 1 = Decimal 15
= F (In Hexadecimal Notation)

For those of you with a mathematical bent, you may notice that the number each finger represents is multiplied by 2 as you go to the left. If we number the fingers:

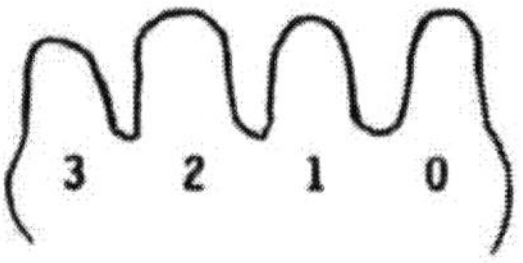

Then the value of each finger is "2 to the power N" where N is the finger number. Let's call a 4-finger hand a "Handlet" (just as a small cigar is a cigarette?)

To prevent confusion, some people write "H" after a hexadecimal number (eg. 10H). The "H" has no hexadecimal convention.

<u>EXERCISE</u>:

What decimal and hexadecimal value do the following arrangement of bits (or fingers) represent?

	DECIMAL	HEXADECIMAL
0010		
0110		
1001		
1010		
1100		

It is important for you to become familiar with the hexadecimal convention, and if you had difficulty with the concept, do read the last few pages again before going on.

Let us examine what happens if we want a number greater than 15 ? Say 16? We would use the next finger on the left, as:

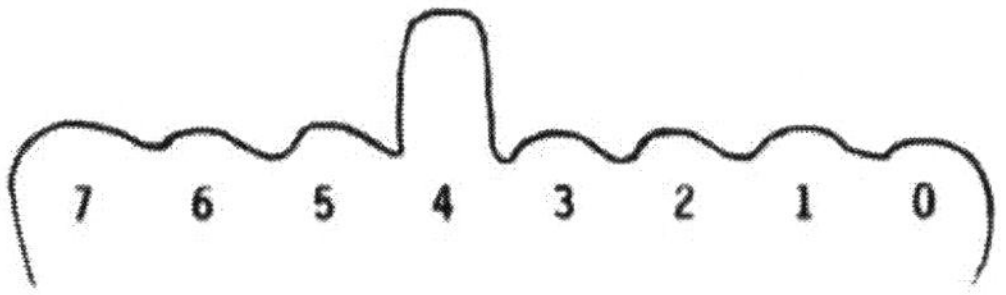

= 16 Decimal = 10H (Hexadecimal)

The reason we write the number as 10H is that we divide the hand in two "4-Bit Handlets". We can therefore easily denote each handlet by one ofthe hexadecimal numbers representing 0 to 15 (0-9 & A-F).

In this way any 8-Bit hand can be written as exactly two hexadecimal handlets:

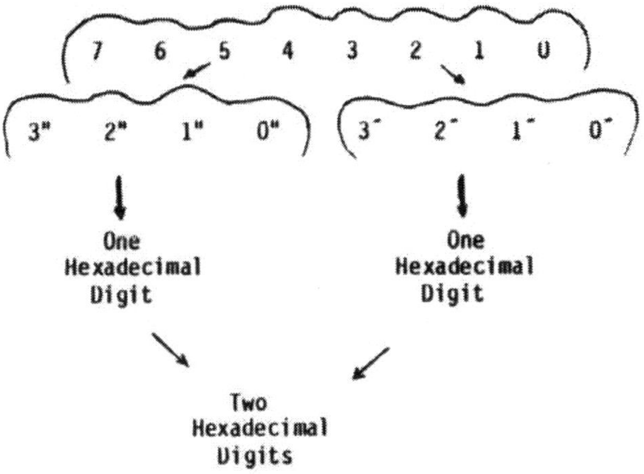

The "Handlets" on the left indicates 16 times as much as the "Handlet" on the right. This is much the same way as in decimal notation. The digit in the "tens" column is worth ten times as much as the digit in the "ones" column.

We convert numbers in decimal format such as 15 automatically to:

15 = (1*10) + 5

This is so automatic that we don't even think about it.

It is exactly the same thing in hexadecimal notation. To convert back from hexadecimal notation to decimal notation, we multiply the hexadecimal number on the left "handlet" by 16. Using the example above:

10H = (1*16) + 0
= 16 Decimal

This is how we are able to count to 255 using only 8 fingers. The maximum is obtained when all fingers are held up:

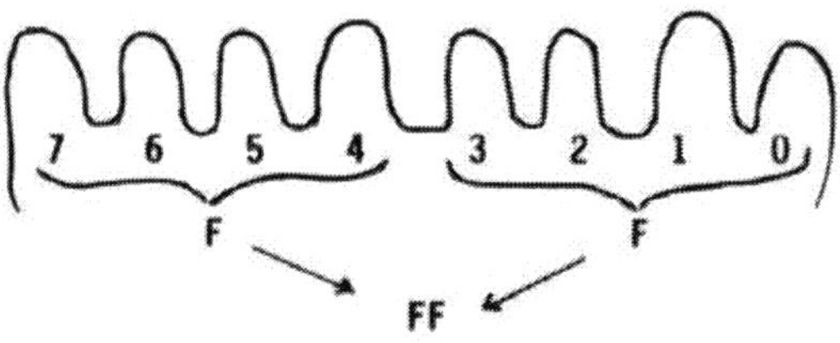

FFH = (F*16) + F
= (15*16) + 15
= 255 (Decimal)

The smallest number is when no fingers are held up:

00H = 0 Decimal

Note that all numbers, from the smallest to the largest require 2 and only 2 digits to define the number.

Try out for yourself any combination of 8 digits and see if you can convert it to hexadecimal notation, and then into decimal notation.

It may seem a little strange and awkward at first, but you will soon get the hang of it.

Also that when you count in hexadecimal, you do the same as in decimal:

Decimal: 26 27 28 29 30 Etc.

Hexadecimal: 26 27 28 29 2A 2B 2C
2D 2E 2F 30 Etc.

The values of the numbers in the decimal and hexadecimal series above have different values of course. Note that after 29H you get 2AH, no 30H!

NEGATIVE NUMBERS

The last chapter showed you how it is possible to represent the numbers 0 to 255 on the fingers of one hand.

I also said that the Z80 chip was mainly designed for operations on one hand (that is 8-bit operations) - in other words, although some instructions allow you the use of two hands)thus giving a number range of 0 - 65,535) most of the work will be done in registers and memory locations that only allow a number range of 00 - FF (in hexadecimal notation).

What about negative numbers?

Life would indeed be limited if we couldn´t represent negative numbers!

Obviously we have to have some representation of negative numbers, so let´s say that a number on our hand is negative if we hold our thumb up. (In computer terminology that is saying that the highest bit - bit 7 - is on).

That means the highest number we can have is not as high as before, because we can no longer say that holding all fingers up will show 255: for a start we have agreed that this will be a negative number. In fact, half the numbers will be negative and half will be positive(depending on whether the thumb is up or not).

The total number range possible on one hand if we allow negative numbers will be from - 128 to +127. (Note that the total number range possible to be represented will still be 256 numbers).

Now comes the crunch: when is a number with the thumb up a large positive number and when is it a negative number?

The answer, as strange as it may seem, is whenever you feel like it!

We have to make a choice: numbers can either be in the range of 0 to 255 or in the range - 128 to +127. They can't be both at the same time! It is up to you, the programmer, to decide which convention you are using at a particular time.

All the instructions will work equally well, whether you choose to let the numbers contained in the registers or memory be all positive or positive and negative.

CHOOSING A REPRESENTATION:

We need a representation of negative numbers, such that, all instructions will work and that when a number is added to its negative we get zero.

Let's think about the number which when added to 1 gives us zero: (we already know that the thumb - bit 7 - will be up)

```
0 0 0 0  0 0 0 1
1 ? ? ?  ? ? ? ?
------------------------
0 0 0 0  0 0 0 0
```

Lets try the number 1 0 0 0 0 0 0 1 - i.e. the same as the positive number but with the thumb up:

```
0 0 0 0  0 0 0 1
1 0 0 0  0 0 0 1
------------------------
1 0 0 0  0 0 1 0
```

This is obviously not the right answer! We need a number that will take that carry from bit 0, and convert it to zeros all along.

You can try to do it yourself, and you will see that the only number which will give us the right answer is 1 1 1 1 1 1 1 1 (FFH in hexadecimal).

```
                    0 0 0 0  0 0 0 1
                    1 1 1 1  1 1 1 1
                    ----------------
          (Carry)   0 0 0 0  0 0 0 0
```

Trying to think of a rule which will produce the negative, it looks as if though we have to get the opposite of the number and add one at the end.

Let's try this rule on another number, such as 3, say:

```
3 =                 0 0 0 0  0 0 1 1
Opposite            1 1 1 1  1 1 0 0
Add 1 =>            1 1 1 1  1 1 0 1        (FDH)
```

Let's add this number to 3 and see what happens:

```
                    0 0 0 0  0 0 1 1
                    1 1 1 1  1 1 0 1
                    ---------------
          (Carry)   0 0 0 0  0 0 0 0          It works!!
```

We have found a way to represent negative numbers!

```
                    - 01 =>   FF
                    - 02 =>   FE
                    - 03 =>   FD and so on.
```

The largest positive number is

```
    0 1 1 1  1 1 1 1  =  7F  =>  127 Decimal
```

And the negative of this is

```
    1 0 0 0  0 0 0 1  =  81  => -127 Decimal
```

The real test of this rule is to see if by applying the rule to a negative number we get back the positive again! Let's try it out on -3 which we worked out above is FDH.

```
Number    1 1 1 1  1 1 0 1
Opposite  0 0 0 0  0 0 1 0
Add 1 =>  0 0 0 0  0 0 1 1        =>   3
```

This is therefore a representation that works! We can apply it any number, whether positive or negative, and get the negative of that number.

16 - Bit Negatives

Exactly the same reasoning applies to 16-bit numbers, except that it is the thumb of the high byte which is set to on to indicate the negativeness of the number. (ie. bit 7 of the high byte).

Convention:

Remember that this is only a convention! You still have to decide at all times whether the numbers you are using are meant to designate numbers in the range 0 to 255 or numbers in the range - 128 to + 127.

Exercise

If 127 (0 1 1 1 1 1 1 1) is the highest positive number which can be represented in this convention, how would you represent - 128?

PROPER NAMES FOR THE CPU'S HANDS AND FEET

The images we have been building up of hands, feet and boxes make the processes easy to visualise and are a good representation of what is going on, but computer buffs tend to look askance if you say things like "... and then the computer shifted its information from its right hand to its left hand."

We will now give you the proper names for the CPU's hands and feet. So that when faced with that situation, you will be able to say:

"LD B,A !"

To start off with, computer buffs refer to the hands and feet of the CPU as "REGISTERS".

We mentioned earlier that the CPU has eight hands: these are called A,B, C,D,E,F,.... In our world, the definition of a hand is something with eight fingers.

The CPU also has two feet: these are named IX and IY. The definition of a foot is anything with 16 toes!

The naming of hands and feet is fairly easy to follow becase if a register has only one letter in its name then it must be a hand (that is, contains 8 bits), while if it has two letters in its name then it must be a foot (that is, have 16 bits).

Did you notice the smooth transition from fingers and toes to bits? We will have you used to computer terminology in no time.

Actually the remaining two hands for the CPU after D,E,F,...are not named "G" and "H" as one would expect but "H" and "L".

The conventional way to represent all these registers is as follows:

A	F
B	C
D	E
H	L
IX	
IY	

Notice that "F" is paired with"A", but after that the rest follow fairly naturally. The reason that registers are paired in this way is that it is sometimes possible to make a foot out of two hands!

After all, if the definition of a foot is something with 16 bits, then maybe we can fake it from time to time and use two 8-bit hands to do the work of a foot. We therefore talk about "Register Pairs" such as BC, DE, and HL.

The reason the register pair "HL" was called "HL" instead of something like "GH" was to help people remember which of the two registers had the high number and which had the low number.

It's as if though you wished to represent the numbers 0 to 100 on your hands and toes. You can easily set up you fingers to represent the numbers 0 through to 10, and similarly with your toes (assuming that you are agile enough). One way you could denote the number 37 in this way would be to count off 3 on your fingers and 7 on your toes. But there has to be some agreement on which is the high number and which is the low number otherwise someone else might think you meant to represent the number 73.

The "H" in "HL" stands for high and the "L" stands for low, so there is no chance of confusion - right?

This diagram of register pairs also serves to indicate which register in the other register pairs contains the hight number:

B in BC

D in DE

Because all the high and lows are treated in the same order.

The feet (IX and IY) also have a special name: they are called "Index Registers". This has a lot to do with the fact that they can be used to organise information in much the same way as a book index is organised.

OK, now that you understand the terminology, here are some special points:

FLAGS:

Please note that "AF" is not usually treated as a register pair. The "F" in this case is used to denote "Flag Register", and we will be dealing with this in a separate chapter.

ALTERNATE REGISTER SET:

I thought that this might be a nice place to mention that the CPU also has a spare set of hands!

Not really so much a spare set of hands (all right, alternate register set, if you want the proper terminology), as a spare set of work gloves.

It's as if though you had a set of stiff plastic gloves, so stiff in fact that they retained the shape of your hand when you took them off. If you had counted off the number 3 on your hand for example and took off your gloves, then the glove would still retain the shape of a hand with the number 3 counted off!

You can no doubt think of uses for such gloves immediately - you could make a note of a number while wearing one set of gloves, swap gloves

CPU

and the old number would still be there when you needed on the other set of gloves!

The other glove is there if you want to use it and it won't forget the impression of your hand when you took it off. Unfortunately you can't just glance down and see what was the number you had retained there. Nor, naturally, can the glove perform any calculations without a hand inside the glove!

You actually have to swap gloves again to be able to use whatever information the gloves retain.

The CPU has a spare set of gloves for each pair of hands (but not for feet - who ever heard of gloves for feet?) But they are not interchangeable between hands, just as you can't put a left glove on a right hand.

The representation of all the registers is now therefore:

```
A - F   <===>  A' - F'
B - C   <===>  B' - C'
D - E   <===>  D' - E'
H - L   <===>  H' - L'
          IX
          IY
```

Whichever set of gloves you are wearing has the same name as the hand it is for, while the spare set is always indicated with the dash symbol.

The instructions still relate to what the hands are doing, not to which pair of gloves you have on. So although we show the spare set with a dash, there are no instructions such as LD A', 1.

The only instructions involving the alternate register set are of the "swap gloves now" type. For example:

```
1.  LD A, (Box #1)    ; load A with contents of
                      ; box #1
2.  EX AF,AF'         ; short for exchange -
                      ; ie. swap gloves on AF
3.  LD A, (Box #2)    ;
                      ;
4.  EX AF,AF'         ; another exchange
                      ;
5.  LD A, (Box #3)    ;
```

You will note that in the previous 5 instructions there are no instructions which have specifically affected the alternate register set but we have without doubt altered their contents.

This example is designed to illustrate the concept of the alternate register set. Try to work out what is happening. Do you know what will be in register "A" after each instruction?

For simplicity's sake, Let's assume that the contents of the three boxes are as follows:

(Box #1) = 1
(Box #2) = 2
(Box #3) = 3

Then the following is what happens after each instruction:

	REGISTER A	REGISTER A'
1.	1	Not known
2.	Not known	1
3.	2	1
4.	1	2
5.	3	2

Really quite simple isn't it?

THIS IS ALL VERY WELL, BUT HOW DO I RUN A MACHINE LANGUAGE PROGRAM?

You have probably heard enough about the CPU and hexadecimal notation, but all this seems so irrelevant. It doesn't explain how you actually (R*U*N) a machine language program.

The Sinclair ZX80 and Sinclair ZX81 are actually running machine language programs all the time! (when they are on). It's just that you are not aware of it. Even when you're not doing anything, just watching the screen, trying to think of what to enter as the first line of your revolutionary Basic program, the Sinclair computer is busy running under the control of a machine language program.

This program is one that is stored in the "ROM" chip and is referred to as 'The Operating System'. For example the part of the program that is running when you're sitting there looking at the screen does the following things:

Scan the keyboard for entry
Note that no key has been pressed
Display the present screen (empty)

Incidentally this is why the screen will flicker when you finally do press a key because the CPU goes on to trying to figure out what to do now that you pressed something. It can't do two things at once, and the one that suffers is the display of the screen.

(Except in the ZX81 SLOW mode - This is because there is another little fellow in the hardware who taps the CPU on the shoulder every so often and reminds the CPU that it's time to display the screen again. Really).

Even when you are running a 'Basic' program, the CPU is still under the instruction of the machine language program. This program is of the 'INTERPRETOR' type: It looks at your next Basic instruction, converts it to machine language, executes that part of the program, and then returns to interpret the next instruction.

All this stops being true when you run your own machine language program!

Total freedom from the operator system! The use of the 'USR' function hands over total control of the CPU to whatever commands you have placed at the USR address.

This can be pretty terrifying as you could lose everything stored in memory if you lose control. One error and you will have to turn the Sinclair off and start again from the beginning.

There are no error messages to catch what you have done, no syntax checking for incorrect statements - so if you make the slightest error, the hours of work you put in to enter your program could be lost!

At the end of this book we have included a 'BASIC' program which will allow you to enter and edit machine language programs. Once you have entered this program on your Sinclair, store it on tape as it is more than likely that you will lose control of your machine language program at least once.

On the other hand do not be afraid to experiment - you cannot damage the computer with any machine language program you enter. The worse that happens is that you may have to turn the Sinclair off and on again.

We will now just whet your appetite with the very simplest possible machine language program. Load the 'BASIC' "Machine Language Editor" found at the back of this book and press "RUN".

The program will ask you for a starting address where you wish to enter your program. Choose an address beyond the end of the space used by the editing program and the variables, such as 17300 for the ZX 80, and then press "NEW LINE".

(Users with Additional Memory could choose any address beyond the space occupied by the program, the display space and the variable storage, such as 19000, say.)

Note ZX 81 : 1K users - due to the extreme space limitations in the ZX 81 version, there is effectively no free memory after the machine code editor program has been entered.

Nonetheless it is possible to enter and run machine language programs by using the printer buffer area which starts at 16444.

Note that in the ZX 81, whether additional memory is available or not, all code poked into free memory will be cleared between 'RUN's. (Even using 'GOTO' does not solve the problem).

The same is true for code poked into the printer buffer area.

Once you have entered the machine code editor program and pressed (RUN), the screen will now show:

```
MEMORY      CODE

16444       00   (ZX 80 users use 17300)
```

Now enter "C" and "9" then press "NEW LINE". the screen should now show:

```
MEMORY      CODE

16444       00   C9  (ZX 80 => 17300)

CHANGES?
```

What the screen display is showing you is the old value at location 16444 (= 00), then the new value at location 16444 (= C9 which you have just entered) and then asks you whether you want to make any changes to what you have just entered.

At this stage you do not want to make any changes, so just press "NEW LINE". (To make changes enter "Y" or "YES" or "YEACH" or any other word that starts with "Y").

Congratulations: you have just entered a one instruction machine machine language program.

What the instruction "C9" means is : RETURN.

It's a little like riding a bicycle for the first time: you really want to be let loose on your own, but as soon as you go a little way you want to "RETURN" to the safety of earth (or operating system as the case may be).

So after you pressed "NEW LINE" above, the program will ask you:

CHANGES? MORE?

The program wants to know if you have any other code you want to enter. Again it's looking for a positive answer and pressing "NEW LINE" will allow you to exit from the program.

The editing program has now finished.

Now we run the machine Language Program:

The program will ask you for the starting address of your machine language program. Enter the starting address where you "POKE"d the machine code:

16444 (OR 17300 FOR ZX 80 USERS)

(Users who chose a different address should make the appropriate change).

Press "New Line" for the running of your first machine language program.

What happened? Why did the screen come up with 16444 or 17300 or whatever address you used as the start?

The answer lies in the way the Sinclair operating system (yes the same one) deals with the "USR" function.

When the operating system encounters the "USR" function it loads the address the user specified into the register pair HL for the ZX 80 - in this case 173000.
The value of "USR", as in

```
        Let A = USR (17300)
```

is the value of the register pair HL on return from the subroutine.

Since our short machine language program did nothing but go and return, the value of HL was unchanged, and the statement

```
        Print USR (S17300)
```

Naturally gave the answer 17300!

This feature of the "USR" function will prove to be a very useful one as it will enable us to monitor what is happening during the running of a machine language program.

In the case of the ZX 81, it is the value of the "BC" register pair which is returned by the "USR" function, but the concept is exactly the same.

Let us enter the following machine language program: (press "Run" if you still have the listing of the "Maching Language Editing Program" on the screen)

	MEMORY	CODE	
ZX 80 USERS ONLY:			
	17300	C9	2B
	17301	00	C9
	Changes?	More?	

The way to enter this short two-instruction program is as follows:

Enter "17300" in response to starting address query
Enter "2B" followed by "New Line" when the screen shows
"17300 C9"
Enter "C9" followed by "New Line" when the screen shows
"17301 00"
Enter "New Line" in response to "Changes?" and to "More?"

The enter "17300" in response to "Start For USR?" and press "New Line".

This time the result will be 17299! This is because the instruction "2B" is "DEC HL" (abbreviation for decrease value of HL by 1).

ZX 81 USERS ONLY:

Enter your program in exactly the same way as above, but change the code to be entered to the following:

	16444	00	0B
	16445	00	C9
Start for USR?	16444		

The concept is again the same, but this time we use an instruction which relates to the "BC" register pair rather than to the "HL" register pair - "0B" means "DEC BC".

You will have noticed a few things about this machine language editing program:

The first column under the heading "Code" shows what is in that location before you make your changes.

The second column under "Code" shows what is in that location after you have tried to make your changes.

The question "Changes?" only came up after you entered "C9" into a location

The following features are some that you would not yet have discovered:

Pressing "New Line" after being shown the contents of a location leaves that location unchanged.

The question "Changes?" will also come up after 20 locations have been displayed. (ZX 81 users program has been designed to show only 10 locations due to the memory limitations of the 1K ZX 81).

Should you answer "Yes" to the question "Any Changes?" then the screen will clear and the program will start again at the first location. The first column under "Code" will now show the contents of the locations as they now exist (i.e. after your changes).

If you have no changes to make, just keep entering "New Line" until you get to the location you want to change, and change the contents in the same way that you have already done.

If you answer "Yes" to the question "More?" the screen will clear and a new set of locations will be displayed.

NOTE:

The last location of the previous page will now be displayed at the top of the page. Don't make the mistake of entering something new at location if you have already got what you want there!

Experiment with looking at different locations and trying to change the contents of different memory locations. Remember you can't hurt the system - the worse that can happen is your screen will go black and will have to turn off the Sinclair and turn it on again.

If you do not want to (R*U*N) a USR program after changing or looking at the contents of memory, enter "XX" as reply to "Start for USR?"

EXERCISE:

Try entering "0" as your starting address (beginning of ROM).
What happens when you try to change the contents of the memory locations?
Why?

EXERCISE:

Try examining the first line of the screen display.
What happens when you change the contents of one of the locations?
What happens when you enter "76"? Why?

INSTRUCTIONS FOR ONE-HANDED

LOADING OPERATIONS

Mnemonic	Bytes	Time Taken	C	Z	PV	S	N	H
					Effect on Flags			
LD Register, Register	1	4	-	-	-	-	-	-
LD Register, Number	2	7	-	-	-	-	-	-
LD A, (Address)	3	13	-	-	-	-	-	-
LD (Address), A	3	13	-	-	-	-	-	-
LD Register, (HL)	1	7	-	-	-	-	-	-
LD A, (BC)	1	7	-	-	-	-	-	-
LD A, (DE)	1	7	-	-	-	-	-	-
LD (HL), Register	1	7	-	-	-	-	-	-
LD (BC), A	1	7	-	-	-	-	-	-
LD (DE), A	1	7	-	-	-	-	-	-
LD Register, (IX+D)	3	19	-	-	-	-	-	-
LD Register, (IY+D)	3	19	-	-	-	-	-	-
LD (IX+D), Register	3	19	-	-	-	-	-	-
LD (IY+D), Register	3	19	-	-	-	-	-	-
LD (HL), Number	2	10	-	-	-	-	-	-
LD (IX+D), Number	4	19	-	-	-	-	-	-
LD (IY+D), Number	4	19	-	-	-	-	-	-

COUNTING OFF NUMBERS

ON ONE HAND

Since everything in the Sinclair CPU is designed around 8-bit hands or 8-bit memory locations, it is obviously of major importance to learn how to count off numbers on one´s hands.

Just which operations are allowed and how easy they are to do is the key to machine language programming.

Imagine for a moment that you are the CPU: obviously like most people, you are right handed and there are things you can do with your right hand that you are not quite so adept at with other hands. The equivalent hand on the CPU is the "A" register.

This is the only one where you can do the complicated tasks of adding and subtracting.

On the other hand (so to speak if you´ll forgive the pun) you can temporarily store what you have in your right hand onto any other hand and vice versa.

Computer boffins refer to this as Register Addressing.

But that is just a big name for saying transfer information from one register to another. Examples are:

```
LD A,B
LD H,E
     and so on.
```

Please note the terminology inolved: "LD" means "Load", "," means "With", and the mnemonic (abbreviation) instruction is read in the same order as an English sentence.

We would thus read out loud something like:

```
LD A,B
```

as "Load A with B". The next example would be read as "Load H with E".

We can swap from one hand to any other hand as we mentioned earlier. The exception that proves the rule is the "F" register which we should not think of as a hand at all. It is as we mentioned earlier the "Flags" register and does not store numbers in the normal sense.

Apart from that exception you can manpulate any hand to any other hand. Even the seemingly stupid instruction "LD A,A" is permitted!

A short shorthand of this is "LD r,r" where "r" represents any 8-bit register except "F".

O.K: we now know we can shuffle information between hands, but that´s not going to do us much good without some original information on those hands.

The second way that we can count off numbers on our hands is for us to specify how many we want the CPU to count off on which hand!

For example, count off 215 on hand "D". I am sure you know enough about the mnemonics by now to be able to write this as:

```
LD D,D7
```

(D7 is the hexadecimal representation of 215).

This is called IMMEDIATE ADDRESSDSING.

(Pretty obvious isn´t it?).

Once again you can do this with any of the registers, with any numbers whatsoever.

(The limitation being of course the size of the nymber you can specify with 8 bits: 0 - 255).

A short shorthand of this is "LD r,n" where "r" indicates any register and "n" any number. The previous convention of one letter =" 8-bits still applies.

Now we're staring to get someplace: we as programmers can now specify which numbers get loaded onto which registers and we can spin them around. But we still haven't learnt how to put any of these numbers away in memory locations, and there are only so many registers!

As soon as we leave the internal registers the CPU is no longer 'At Home'.We therefore call putting something away in a memory location "External Addressing".

We showed you very briefly an example of this when we were doing the time difference exercise:

```
LD A, (Box #3)
```

The general mnemonic for this is:

```
LD A, (nn)
```

Don't forget that in our shorthand the brackets imply "The Contents Of".

Note two things about this:
1. You can only do it with Register A
2. You have to supply the number of the box as a 16-bit number.

The reverse instruction is also valid. This is one thing you will notice about the Z80 - there is a certain symmetry about the instruction set:

```
LD (nn),A
```

Do notice that these instructions only apply to Register "A" - there will be times when you will wish for such instructions involving the other registers.

Let us pause here for a second and consider what these two instructions actually mean and do for us.

In the first place, the maximum number that can be defined by the number nn is a little over 64,000. This means that the maximum memory possibly reached by this instruction is only 64K! In fact on the Sinclair machines, because of the hardware construction everything over 32K is not available to the user.

This means that all the memory - ROM, Program, Display, and free memory - have to fit in 32K:

The first 8K are reserved for the ROM.
The second 8K are a copy of the 1st 8K as a result of the hardware design
The last 16K are the maximum RAM possible.

The instruction "LD A, (nn)" - which is read as "Load A with the contents of location nn" - is a very powerful instruction. It enables us to "Read" the contents of any memory location, whether in ROM, or RAM.

You can use this instruction to explore to your heart's desire, even to a location where there is no memory - e.g. to try to see what is beyond the 1K RAM memory even if you do not have additional memory. You will be surprised - it is not all zeros!

The reverse instruction "LD (nn),A" - which is read as "Load the contents of memory location nn with A" - will attempt to write to any memory location as well, but will be restricted by the physical limitations:
You can't write to a location that can't store that information, such as memory beyond the size of your system or into ROM space.

Another consequence of this instruction is that we have to know at the time of writing the program which memory location we wish to examine or write into. The abbreviation "nn" means a definite number - e.g. 17100 - and not a variable.

You can't use this instruction in the machine language equivalent of a "FOR - NEXT" loop. The main use for this instruction is therefore for setting aside particular memory locations as variable storage. E.g. define 17000 = Speed
17001 = Height
17002 = Fuel Left
In a lunar lander type program.

You could therefore plan a program where you got the fuel left, decreased it, and stored the new amount of fuel back into that location. You will know at the time of writing your program the address of that memory location which serves to act as a variable.

Let us be clear about this. Location 17002 is not a variable. It is only a memory location which you use to store certain information.

When writing your program you would therefore write something like

```
LD A,(Fuel)
```

and when you or the assembler got to specifying the actual machine code for this instruction you would replace "Fuel" by the hexadecimal address of the memory location you specified.

But what if we don't know the exact address of the memory location where the information we seek is. Suppose we can only calculate where that information is going to be? Because we need 16-bits to specify the address of any memory location, we would need to store it in a 16-bit register: this means one of the register pairs BC, DE, or HL, or one of the Index Registers IX or IY.

One way we can do this is to have one of the register pair contain the address of the memory location. Because the register contain the information and because we don't have the address directly we call this form of addressing Register Indirect Addressing.

The mnemonic abbreviations for these are

```
LD  r,(HL)
LD  A,(BC)
LD  A,(DE)
```

The English reading of these instructions is

"Load the register with the contents of the memory location pointed to by HL"

"Load A with the contents of the memory location pointed to by BC"

"Load A with the contents of the memory location pointed to by DE".

Note that by using "HL" as the pointer to our memory location we can load to any register - even H or L, as strange as that may sound - but that using BC or DE we can only load into the A register.

This is because the HL register pair is the favoured register pair in the same way that the A register is the favoured single register.

Once again there is a symmetry to these instructions and we can store information into memory locations in a similar way:

```
LD  (HL),r
LD  (BC),A
LD  (DE),A
```

This is still called "Register Indirect Addressing" whichever direction the information flows in.

Alternatively we could use the Index Registers IX and IY to point to the memory location. This is where we will find out why they are called Index Registers and I am sure it will come as no surprise to you that this kind of pointing is called INDEXED ADDRESSING.

The reason that they are called Index Registers is that we can use them as pointers to an entire table of items, such as the 1st item, the 10th item, the 137th item and so on.

The short shorthand is:

```
LD  r,(IX + d)
LD  r,(IY + d)
```

"r" is again any register, and "d" is the "displacement" from the address pointed to by IX or IY. (Don't get the use of "d" confused - we don't mean register "D" but d = displacement).

The number "d" is an 8-bit number which has to be specified at the time of programming and cannot be a variable. This is the weakness of this particular instruction and means that its use is usually limited to reading and writing tables containing data.

The symmetrical instruction is also available:

```
LD  (IX + d),r
LD  (IY + d),r
```

If this particular mode of addressing sounds a little complicated, don't worry: it is not a very commonly used instruction and you are unlikely to need it in your first few programs.

The Z80 chip used in the Sinclair Computers is nothing if not versatile, and you can combine some of the ways of loading numbers we described above.

For example, you can combine immediate addressing (i.e. specifying the number you want loaded) with external addressing (i.e. specifying the address to be loaded by using a register pair).

This is called - surprise,surprise - "IMMEDIATE EXTERNAL ADDRESSING".

Unfortunately you can only use the HL Register Pair and the short shorthand is therefore:

```
LD  (HL),n
```

This is useful as you can directly fill a memory location without first having to load the value in a register.

A similar combination is possible with the Index Registers, called "IMMEDIATE INDEXED ADDRESSING".

This is of more limited use, and the abbreviated form for these instructions are:

```
LD  (IX + d),n
LD  (IY + d),n
```

USING THESE INSTRUCTIONS IN A MACHINE LANGUAGE PROGRAM

Let´s try to put some of these "LD" instructions into practice.

We know from the previous chapters that after returning from a ´USR´ machine language program the value of the ´USR´ is the contents of HL. Let´s run the following program:

MEMORY	CODE

FOR ZX 80 USERS:

17300	00	2E
17301	00	00
17302	00	C9
Changes?	More?	

FOR ZX 81 USERS:

16444	00	0E
16445	00	00
16446	00	C9

From now on, we will no longer be showing you machine language programs in this way as it is a cumbersome method and does not allow you, the user, to understand the point of the program.

We assume that by now you have enough familiarity with the basic "Machine Language Editor" to be able to enter program. We will therefore be showing all of our programs as follows:

```
ZX 80 Version          !     ZX81 Version

2E  00      LD  L,0    !     0E  00     LD   C,0
C9          Ret        !     C9         Ret
```

This notation gives you the machine codes on the left side and the

Z80 assembly mnemonics in the right hand column. It also indicates very clearly which instructions require only a single byte (such as return) and which instructions require 2 bytes,etc. (Some instructions on the Z80 can take up to 4 bytes!).

The other point is that we shall try to make all our program independent of origin so that it does not matter what you specify as your starting address.

Nonetheless remember that these programs are designed to be entered with the "Machine Language Editor" program at the back of the book or any other loading program you may design yourself.

Before running this program what do you expect the result to be?
The program sets the "L" register in the register pair HL to zero, and you know that HL starts off with the address of the program, say 17100.

Will the answer be	ZX 80:	ZX81:
	A. 0000	A. 0000
	B. 17300	B. 16444
	C. 16896	C. 16384

Now run the program. Was the answer what you expected it to be?

If you are unclear about why the answer was what it was go back and reread the chapter on "The Way Computers Count".

Now try running the following program:

```
ZX 80 Version          !     ZX81 Version

26  00    LD H,0       !     06  00   LD  B,0
2E  00    LD L,0       !     0E  00   LD  C,0
C9        Ret          !     C9       Ret
```

This will give you the expected result of 0 as HL=0 (both registers H and L have been set to 0) or BC=0, depending on which program you run.

EXERCISE:

You might like to try a few fancy tricks, such as loading A with a number, transferring to L, setting H to 0 and so on.

EXERCISE:

ZX 80 users only : an interesting point to think about - what happens when you set H to 200 and L to 0?

$$200 * 256 + 0 = 51{,}200$$

You won't get the answer of 51,200.
Why?

FLAGS AND THEIR USES

Flags are those nice buntings you can wave on state occasions ... wrong!

In Machine Language, the word "Flag" implies "Indicator" - a flag is something you put up if you wish to indicate to someone else that a certain condition exists.

The obvious example is in boating where you rig up a flag to indicate distress, country, piracy or whatever.

The reason we use flags in machine language is to give the programmer information about the status of the number in the CPU's right hand (the 'A' Register) or information about the last calculation just performed.

You will remember that one of the CPU's registers is dedicated to be a Flags Register. You may also have noticed at the start of the last chapter a table summarising the various instructions to be discussed in that chapter, and that part of that table was devoted to the effect each instruction would have on the flags. (Fortunately none of the instructions discussed in the last chapter affected any of the flags).

The flag whose functioning is easiest to understand is the ZERO FLAG.

This flag will be run up the flag-pole if the contents of the 'A' register is zero.

There are many important decisions which will depend on whether 'A' is zero. Note that the zero flag is either on or off. You can't have an in-between result (shade of 'a little pregnant') so that you would only need one bit to define the zero flag.

The same is true for all the other flags as well. They are either on or off and require only one bit.

THE DIFFERENT KINDS OF FLAGS:

The "F" register is a regular 8-bit register and could therefore accomodate 8 different flags. In practice however the designers could only think of 6 flags!

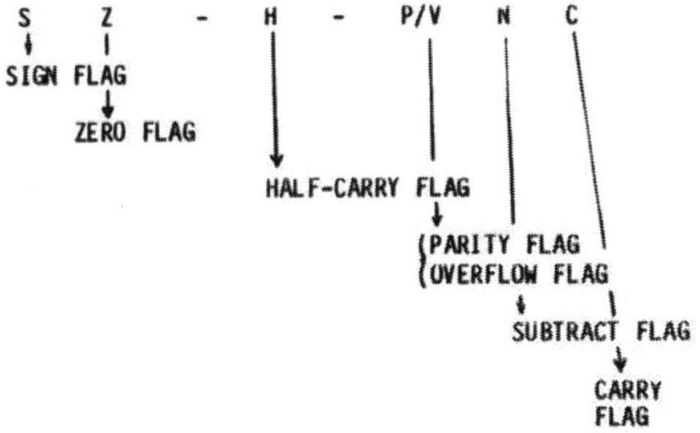

Actually the designers thought of seven flags, but decided that one bit could serve as both flags: the parity/overflow flag.

Let us now look at each of these flags in detail:

ZERO FLAG:

This is the flag we have already discussed above. Its application is obvious, and the flag is usually set after an arithmetic operation as it serves to indicate the contents of the "A" register.

N
C
CPL

Note carefully however that it is possible to have the "A" register contain 0 and for the zero flag not be set. This could easily happen by using the

```
LD    A,0
```

instruction.
We have mentioned above that none of the 8-bit load instructions had any effect on any of the flags.

The zero flag is also set if the result of the "Rotate and Shift" group of instructions results in a zero.

As well, the zero flag is the only visible result of some testing instructions, such as the "Bit Testing" group of instructions. In those cases the zero flag is put on if the bit tested is zero.

SIGN FLAG:

The sign flag is very similar to the zero flag and operates on very much the same set of instructions (with the major point of departure being the "Bit Testing" group where the concept of a negative bit is somewhat meaningless in any case).

In the case of the sign flag, it will be set if the result of the arithmetic operation is negative.

CARRY FLAG:

This is one of the more important flags available in assembly language, for without it the results of assembly language arithmetic would be totally meaningless.

The point to remember is that assembly language instructions always refer to either 8-bit or 16-bit numbers.

This means that the numbers we are dealing with can be either :

```
 8-bit   ==>    0 - 255
16-bit   ==>    0 - 65536
```

Consider the situation where we subtract

```
            200
          - 201
            ---
Result =    255!
```

This is a direct consequence of only having a limited number range available, and the same thing can obviously happen with 16-bit numbers.

The carry flag can also be set by addition operations.

It is therefore convenient to think of the carry bit as the 9th bit of the "A" register:

No.	"C"	Number in Bit Form
132	-	1 0 0 0 0 1 0 0
+ 135	-	1 0 0 0 0 1 1 1
------		----------------------
267	1	0 0 0 0 1 0 1 1

But as we do not have 9 bits, the "A" register would contain the number "Decimal 11" and the carry would be on (i.e. = 1).

You can see that on subtraction borrowing from a 9th bit would leave a "1" there as well.

MACHINE LANGUAGE EQUIVALENT OF "IF ... THEN ..."

The equivalent in a basic program is:

If A=0 then ...

where what follows can be "Let ..."
or "Goto ..."
or "Gosub ..."

Exactly the same kind of decision can be programmed in Machine Language (except for the ´Let ...´). Instead of saying "If A=0", we merely look at the zero flag: If it is on, then we know A=0.

The three flags we have been considering to date are in the main the only ones which allow us to execute a branch or a choice in the next instruction to be executed.

The format of such instruction is as follows:
For example:

```
        JP   cc,End
```

Where ´JP´ is the mnemonic for ´Jump´ and ´End´ is a convenient label. The instruction is read in English as "Jump on condition cc to end".

The condition "cc" could be any of:

```
         Z  (  => Zero)
        NZ  (  => Not Zero)
         P  (  => Positive)
         M  (  => Minus)
         C  (  => Carry Set)
        NC  (  => No Carry)
```

The other three flags tend not to be of so much use in every day programming. They are:

<u>PARITY / OVERFLOW FLAG:</u>

This flag acts as the parity flag for some instructions, and as the overflow flag on others, but there is rarely any confusion as the two types of operations do not commonly occur together.

The parity side of it comes into effect during logical operations and is set if there is an even number of bits in the result. We deal with this in greater detail in the chapter on logical operations.

The overflow is a warning device that tells you that the arithmetic operation you have just performed may not fit into the 8-bits. Rather than actually telling you that the result needed a 9th bit, this tells you that the 8th bit changed as a result of the operation!

In the example above, adding 132 and 135, the 8th bit was "1" prior to the addition and "0" afterwards, so that the overflow would have been set. But the overflow would also be set by adding:

```
      64       0 1 0 0  0 0 0 0
  +   65       0 1 0 0  0 0 0 1
  -------      ----------------------
     129       1 0 0 0  0 0 0 1
```

SUBTRACTION FLAG:

This flag is set if the last operation was a subtraction!

HALF-CARRY FLAG:

This flag is set in a manner similar to the carry flag but only in the case of an overflow or borrow from the 5th bit instead of from the 9th bit!

Both the subtract flag and the half-carry flag are of use only in "Binary Coded Decimal" arithmetic, and we deal with these flags in the chapter on "BCD Arithmetic".

COUNTING UP AND DOWN

In the last chapter we examined the concept of flags, and in the chapter before we found out how the CPU gets certain numbers onto its fingers and toes.

Let us now examine the simple possible way to manipulate numbers on one's fingers: we can increase the number represented on our fingers or we can decrease the number represented.

This is a pretty rudimentary arithmetic, but it gets beyond loading specific numbers onto your fingers. The action of counting up is essentially: whatever number you have on your fingers, increase by one.

This can be used in such ordinary situations as census taking or monitoring the traffic at a particular intersection.

COUNTING UP

It is possible on the Z80 to increase the count on the fingers of every single hand the CPU has. This is what we mean by the general mnemonic:

```
INC r
```

"INC" is read in English as "Increase" and is therefore fairly self-explanatory.

It is also possible to increase the count held on the toes of any of the feet (including the register pairs, which are not really feet, as we saw).

This increasing of the count on our toes is written as:

```
INC rr
INC IX
INC IY
```

Where "rr" denotes a register pair, such as ´BC´, ´DE´, or ´HL´.

Note again the simple way we have of denoting which operations are using 8-bit numbers and which are using 16-bit numbers:

The 8-bit numbers are denoted by a single letter, while
The 16-bit numbers are denoted by two letters.

But the "Counting Up" instruction is in fact even more powerful than this might indicate. It is possible to increase the count of any memory location if we are able to specify its address using the Index Registers or the ´Favoured Register Pair´, HL:

```
INC (IX + d)
INC (IY + d)
INC (HL)
```

(Where ´d´ is the displacement - not the Register!)

IMPORTANT NOTE:

Remember carefully our convention of reading brackets:

Brackets ==> ´Contents of´

This is very important as there is a lot of similarity between the instructions

```
INC   HL
INC   (HL)
```

But a world of difference in their execution.

The first would be read as "Increase HL" while the second would be read as "Increase the contents of the location whose address is HL". (This second reading is often abbreviated to "Increase the contents of HL".)

As long as you remember the rules of the menmonic abbreviations you will be saved from this kind of confusion. Let us examine how each operates, and let´s assume that HL = 16396.

INC HL: Look at HL. Increase the count on its fingers by one.
Result:
HL = 16397

INC (HL): Look at HL. Find the memory location referred to by this number. Increase the count in that location by one.
Result:
HL = 16396
(16396) = (16396) + 1

These are significantly different operations. Note also that while "INC HL" is an instruction acting on a 16-bit number, "INC (HL)" is an instruction which acts on an 8-bit number only - the number stored in location 16396!

DECREASING THE COUNT:

The symmetrical nature of the Z80 instruction set would almost certainly ensure that everything you can increase you can also decrease, and this is indeed the case:

```
DEC r
DEC rr
DEC IX
DEC IY
DEC (HL)
DEC  (IX + d)
DEC  (IY + d)
```

The mnemonic "DEC" is read in English as "Decrease", and the same careful attention to the use of brackets must by applied here.

EFFECT ON FLAGS:

Because the increase or decrease instructions which operate on 8-bit numbers affect every flag except the carry flag, this is a very good place to review the operation of the flags.

(Note that the increase and decrease instructions which operate on 16-bit numbers do not effect any of the flags!)

SIGN: This flag will be set (=1) if bit 7 of the 8-bit result is 1.

ZERO: This flag will be set (=1) if the 8-bit result is zero.

OVERFLOW: This flag will be set (=1) if the contents of bit 7 of the 8-bit number is changed by the operation.

HALF-CARRY: This flag will be set (=1) if there is a carry into or a borrow from bit 4 of the 8-bit number.

NEGATE: This flag is set if the last instruction was a subtraction. Thus it is not set (=0) for "Inc", and set (=1) for "Dec".

SUGGESTED EXERCISES:

Use the "Load", "Inc" and "Dec" group of instructions to return the numbers you want as a result of the "USR" operation.

This will give you familiarity with these instructions.

INSTRUCTIONS FOR ONE-HANDED ARITHMETICAL OPERATIONS

MNEMONIC	BYTES	TIME TAKEN	C	Z	PV	S	N	H
Add Register	1	4	#	#	#	#	0	#
Add Number	2	7	#	#	#	#	0	#
Add (HL)	1	7	#	#	#	#	0	#
Add (IX+d)	3	19	#	#	#	#	0	#
Add (IY+d)	3	19	#	#	#	#	0	#
ADC Register	1	4	#	#	#	#	0	#
ADC Number	2	7	#	#	#	#	0	#
ADC (HL)	1	7	#	#	#	#	0	#
ADC (IX+d)	3	19	#	#	#	#	0	#
ADC (IY+d)	3	19	#	#	#	#	0	#
Sub Register	1	4	#	#	#	#	1	#
Sub Number	2	7	#	#	#	#	1	#
Sub (HL)	1	7	#	#	#	#	1	#
Sub (IX+d)	3	19	#	#	#	#	1	#
Sub (IY+d)	3	19	#	#	#	#	1	#
SBC Register	1	4	#	#	#	#	1	#
SBC Number	2	7	#	#	#	#	1	#
SBC (HL)	1	7	#	#	#	#	1	#
SBC (IX+d)	3	19	#	#	#	#	1	#
SBC (IY+d)	3	19	#	#	#	#	1	#
CP Register	1	4	#	#	#	#	1	#
CP Number	2	7	#	#	#	#	1	#
CP (HL)	1	7	#	#	#	#	1	#
CP (IX+d)	3	19	#	#	#	#	1	#
CP (IY+d)	3	19	#	#	#	#	1	#

(The column headings C, Z, PV, S, N, H appear under the heading "EFFECT ON FLAGS".)

FLAGS NOTATION:

# Indicates flag is altered by operation
0 Indicates flag is set to 0
1 Indicates flag is set to 1
- Indicates flag is unaffected

ONE HAND ARITHMETIC

One hand arithmetic is just our reminder that all of these operations in this chapter involve only 8-bits and all of them must be carried out through our right hand.

It seems that only our right hand knows how to add or subtract!

This fact is so ingrained in the Z80 machine language menmonics that the abbreviation "A" is even omitted. For example to add "B" to "A", we would normally expect to see

```
ADD A,B
```

But in fact the mnemonic is

```
ADD B.
```

Despite this limitation on arithmetical instructions, the Z80 language is very versatile in what we can actually add to whatever number we have on our right hand:

Add r	Add any single register to A
Add n	Add any 8-bit number to A
Add (HL)	Add the 8-bit number in the box whose address is given by HL
Add (IX + d)	Add the 8-bit number in the box whose address is given by IX+d
Add (IY +d)	Add the 8-bit number in the box whose address is given by IY+d

You can appreciate that this is an extremely versatile range of possible numbers we can add to whatever number is stored in A - any number, any register and virtually any way we care to define a memory location.

The one that is missing is

```
Add (nn)
```

where we define the address in the course of the program.

As a result the only way to get such an instruction would be to write:

```
LD HL,nn
ADD (HL)
```

Note also the favoured role of the HL register again. We cannot specify the memory location using the BC or DC register pairs.

The other limitation implicit in all this is also the limitation of 8-bit numbers:

```
LD A,80H
ADD 81H
```

will give a result of only 1 in ˝A˝ but the carry flag will be set to indicate the result did not fit in.

(If the hexadecimal arithmetical confuses you, it˝s really just the same as ordinary arithmetic but you go to ˝F˝ instead of stopping at ˝9˝:

```
  80
+ 81
----
 101H  as 8+8=16 ==> 10H)
```

There is therefore the very useful instruction "ADC" which we read as "ADD WITH CARRY".

This is exactly the same as the "ADD" instruction, with the same range of numbers which can be added to ˝A˝, except that the carry is added on (if it is set).

This makes it possible to add numbers greater than 255 together, by a chaining operation:

E.G. To add 1000 (i.e. 03E8H) to 2000 (i.e. 07D0H) and store the result in BC:

```
LD  A,E8H    ;Lower Part 1st No.
ADD D0H      ;Lower Part 2nd No.
LD  C,A      ;Store Result in C
LD  A,03H    ;Higher Part 1st No.
ADC 07H      ;Higher Part 2nd No.
LD  B,A      ;Store Result in B
```

After the first addition (E8 + D0) we will have the carry set (because result was greater than FF) and A containing B8 (check this for yourselves!).

The second addition (3 + 7) will yield not 0AH (= 10 Decimal) as might seem on the surface but 0BH (= 11 Decimal) because of the carry.

The final result is therefore 0BB8H = 3000! This chaining could go on to take care of any size number rather than simply in a register pair.

8-Bit Subtraction:

This is exactly the same as 8-bit addition. Two sets of commands exist, one for ordinary subtraction, and one for subtraction with carry:

```
SUB s  -  SUBTRACT S
SBC s  -  SUBTRACT S WITH CARRY
```

The notation ˝S˝ is meant to denote the same range of possible operands as for the Add instruction.

COMPARING TWO 8-BIT NUMBERS:

Let us step back from machine language for a moment and consider exactly what it is we mean when we compare two numbers:

We know what happens when the two numbers being compared are the same - they are ˝equal˝. One way to denote this in an arithmetical format would be to say that the difference between the two numbers was zero.

What if the number being compared is greater than the first number (comparison does imply relating two numbers: we compare a number with what we already have on our fingers). Then the result after subtracting the new number will be negative.

Similarly if the new number is smaller, then the difference will be positive.

We can use these concepts to devise a system of comparisons in machine language. All we need are the flags and the subtract operation. Suppose we wish to compare a range of numbers with 5, say:

```
LD A,5          ;Number we have
SUB N           ;Number being compared
```

Then we will have the following results -

If N = 5 Zero Flag set, Carry flag not set
If N < 5 Zero Flag not set, Carry not set
If N > 5 Zero Flag not set, Carry flag set.

It is therefore clear that the test for equality will be the zero flag, and the test for ">" will be the carry flag. (The test for "<" is the absence of both flags).

The only inconvenience of this method is that the contents of 'A' have been altered by the operation.

Fortunately we have the "CP s" operation. This is read in English as "Compare". Note that it can only compare what we already have in the 'A' register; the range of possible numbers to be compared are the same as for addition.

"Compare" is exactly the same as "Subtract" except that the contents of 'A' are unchanged. The only effect is therefore on the flags.

INSTRUCTION FOR TWO-HANDED LOADING OPERATIONS

MNEMONIC	BYTES	TIME TAKEN	C	Z	PV	S	N	H
LD Reg Pair, Number	3	10	-	-	-	-	-	-
LD IX, Number	4	14	-	-	-	-	-	-
LD IY, Number	4	14	-	-	-	-	-	-
LD (Address), BC or DE	4	20	-	-	-	-	-	-
LD (Address), HL	3	16	-	-	-	-	-	-
LD (Address), IX	4	20	-	-	-	-	-	-
LD (Address), IY	4	20	-	-	-	-	-	-
LD BC or DE, (Address)	4	20	-	-	-	-	-	-
LD HL, (Address)	3	16	-	-	-	-	-	-
LD IX, (Address)	4	20	-	-	-	-	-	-
LD IY, (Address)	4	20	-	-	-	-	-	-

(EFFECT ON FLAGS: C Z PV S N H)

FLAGS NOTATION:

- \# Indicates flag is altered by operation
- 0 Indicates flag is set to 0
- 1 Indicates flag is set to 1
- \- Indicates flag is unaffected

MANIPULATING NUMBERS
WITH TWO HANDS

In the preceding chapters we have seen just how agile the CPU can be in manipulating numbers on one hand.

His mathematical ability is such that he can also perform very complex calculations involving large numbers with only one hand.

But there are points where it it impossible to specify everything one wants with just 8-bit numbers. If we were limited to just the range of 0 - 255 of the 8-bit numbers our computer would indeed be a very limited machine.

The most glaring example of needing 16-bit numbers is specifying the address of a memory location. We implied that such a manipulation would be possible when we discussed instructions such as LD A,(HL).

The slow way of doing things would be to load each individual register in the register pair, as we did in the exercises of Chaper 7.

Fortunately for us there are some (but only a few) instructions on the Z80 chip which allow us to manipulate 16-bit numbers. In this chapter we shall be dealing solely with loading 16-bit numbers, while the next chapter will deal with 16-bit arithmetic.

SPECIFYING ADDRESSES WITH 16-BIT NUMBERS:

Please note that all addresses must be specified by a 16-bit number.

You just can't specify an address with only 8-bits, even if it is only addresses from 0 to 255. The way the CPU works, it's not an address unless it is 2 bytes of 8 bits each.

We implied this when we used the short shorthand of

LD A, (NN)

So also remember that 16-bits numbers are stored in register pairs high number first (check again with Chapter 5. -"HL" stands for "High"; "Low").

STORING 16-BIT NUMBERS IN MEMORY:

There is one facet of Z80 design which is very difficult to explain or justify:

When loading 16-bit numbers into memory, the reverse convention from that of register pairs is used.

The low bit is always stored first in memory.

Let us consider a situation where we place the contents of HL into memory:

BEFORE:

		LOCATION	CONTENTS
		17100	00
H	L	17101	00
01	02	17102	00

Let us assume that HL contains the number 258 decimal = 0102H. The memory locations are all empty.

AFTER:

		LOCATION	CONTENTS
		17100	02
H	L	17101	01
01	02	17102	00

The convention with 16-bit numbers stored in memory (and in program listings) is that the low bit is always stored first.

There is no justification for that decision except to say that this was what the designers of the Z80 came up with and we now have to live with it.

Please be sure to read this carefully and make sure that you are familiar with this reversal of convention. It is likely to be the single most important source of errors in programs:

In registers: high bit stored first
In memory and programs: low bit stored first.

It is not something that can be glossed over and ignored as every time you deal with a 16-bit instruction in machine code you will need to think carefully about the order of the low and high bits.

Do not however feel put off by this - life on the Z80 would be virtually impossible without 16-bit instructions and it's a price we have to pay.

LOADING 16-BIT NUMBERS:

The 16-bit load group at its simplest comprises of loading a 16-bit number in the register pair. The general mnemonic abbreviation is

```
LD  rr, nn
```

Once again we are using the notation of 2 letters to indicate a 16-bit number. "rr" means any register pair, "nn" any 16-bit number.

For those of you without the benefit of an assembler - that is if you have to convert the mnemonics into code by hand using the tables at the back of the book - then the discussion we had of the order of the 16-bit numbers in memory becomes crucial.

Even if you do have an assembler, you should be aware of these reversals of order to enable you to "read" the code when peeking into memory.

Let us look at a specific example:

```
          Load HL with 258
the mnemonic for this is
          LD HL,0102H
```

The instruction for ˝LD HL,nn˝ is, as you will find at the end of the book,

```
          21 XX XX
```

This means that the number 0102H needs to be inserted in place of the ˝XX XX˝. But because of the reversal rule, we do not enter this as 0102H.

The proper instruction is therefore:

```
          21 02 01
```

In our examples we will show you this as

```
    21  02  01          LD  HL, 0102H ( = 258)
```

You may not have problems entering our programs, but you need to be familiar with this when you write your own programs.

<u>OTHER 16-BIT LOAD INSTRUCTIONS:</u>

As well as being able to load 16-bit numbers directly into the register pairs we can also load 16-bit numbers directly into the index registers (which are both 16-toe feet, as you will remember).

```
          LD  IX,  nn
          LD  IY,  nn
```

We can also manipulate information between a register pair and two successive locations in memory. (This is the 16-bit equivalent of loading the information from a single register into a single memory location).

The general instructions are

```
LD (nn), dd
LD (nn), IX
LD (nn), IY
```

Remember that brackets are the shorthand for "Contents Of", so that the last instruction would be read as "Load the contents of memory location nn with register IY".

Because we are dealing with 16-bit numbers, we are actually loading the memory location specified and the following memory location into the register pair. It is not necessary to specify both addresses (because the CPU can figure out the address of the second location) but be careful not to confuse 8-bit operations with 16-bit operations.

The reciprocal nature of many of the instructions is also apparent here, and we can also load a register pair of index register with whatever is in a specific pair of memory locations:

```
LD dd, (nn)
LD IX, (nn)
LD IY, (nn)
```

EXERCISE:

ZX80 version: run the following short program entering it through the editing program -

```
2A 0C 40        LD HL, (16396)
C9              RET
```

We know from the ZX80 manual that 16396 and 16397 contain the address for the start of the screen display. If you now "RUN" this program by entering

Start for USR?   17300

(assuming you have loaded it at 17300), you will receive as an answer the address of the display start.

Now try running the following program:

```
2A 0E 40        LD HL, (16398)
C9              RET
```

This will give you the address at the end of the screen. Is this what you expected? Can you work out why the screen is only 25 characters long?

<u>**NOTE VERY CAREFULLY THAT THE NUMBERS ARE ENTERED LOW BYTE FIRST AND YOU WOULD GET A TOTALLY ERRONEOUS ANSWER IF YOU WERE TO ENTER THEM THE OTHER WAY ROUND.**</u>

ZX81 VERSION:

In the ZX81 case the screen start is also defined by the contents of memory locations 16396 and 16397 but this time we want the result to be returned in register pair "BC":

```
ED 4B  0C 40          LD BC, (16396)
C9                    RET
```

In the ZX81, we know that once the program is finalised the position of the screen start is fixed and we only need to determine this once in each program.

On the other hand, if the system does not have a minimum of 3-1/4K of memory, the locations where the variables are stored will move around and the start of the variable file can be found by

```
ED 4B 10 40           LD BC, (16400)
C9                    RET
```

Note that "LD BC, (nn)" is a four-byte instruction!

MANIPULATING THE STACK

You may recall the image we developed in the beginning of the book of the stack where the CPU was able to keep information without having to remember the address of that particular information.

One of the advantages, possibly inadvertent, of the stack operations is that we can only PUSH and POP information in 16-bit lots. This is because the stack is primarily designed to remember addresses and we need to specify addresses as 16-bit numbers.

The general instructions for pushing information to the stack are

```
PUSH rr
PUSH IX
PUSH IY
```

And the general instruction for popping information back from the stack are

```
POP rr
POP IX
POp IY
```

This is an exceptionally simple instruction, and you will note the lack of need to specify an address.

For the ordinary register pairs - i.e. not the index registers - these instructions are only a single byte long and therefore very economical in terms of programming space.

PUSH instructions are also not destructive: that is, the 16-bit register still contains the same information after the PUSHES.

Note that because we can PUSH any register pair and POP any register pair, the register you POP may not be the same as the one you PUSHED!

For example

```
              PUSH  BC
              POP   HL
```

The effect of these two instructions is to leave the contents of the BC register unchanged but set the HL register to whatever the contents of the BC register were at the time of the push instruction.

This effectively adds an instruction of the type

```
              LD rr, rr'
```

from the 16-bit load group which was conspicuously missing. As each of the PUSH and POP instructions for the register pair is only one byte long, the cost in terms of memory is not expensive.

The other extra is that we are able to PUSH or POP the register pair AF! This is one of the few instructions where AF is treated as a register pair, but it is obviously sensible because there are many times when we would like to preserve the contents of the flags.

<u>MOVING THE STACK AROUND</u>:

As you know, the real strength of the PUSH and POP instructions is that we do not have to think about the addresses.

But you will agree that it does not necessarily make sense that the same area of memory should serve as a stack if you have 16K of memory as if you only have 1K.

The way the CPU actually keeps track of the address of the stack is by means of a "stack pointer", whcih can be thought of as a 16-bit register. We did not include it in our discussion of registers because it is not a register that can be manipulated in the same manner as the other registers.

The main thing one would want to do with the stack pointer is to define its position in memory, and that is exactly the type of instruction that is available.

INSTRUCTION FOR STACK OPERATIONS

MNEMONIC	BYTES	TIME TAKEN	C	Z	PV	S	N	H
PUSH Reg Pair	1	11	-	-	-	-	-	-
PUSH 1X or 1Y	2	15	-	-	-	-	-	-
POP Reg Pair	1	10	-	-	-	-	-	-
POP 1X or 1Y	2	14	-	-	-	-	-	-
LD SP, Address	3	10	-	-	-	-	-	-
LD SP,(Address)	3	20	-	-	-	-	-	-
LD SP, HL	1	6	-	-	-	-	-	-
LD SP, IX or IY	2	10	-	-	-	-	-	-

(C, Z, PV, S, N, H: EFFECT ON FLAGS)

FLAGS NOTATION:

\# Indicates flag is altered by operation
0 Indicates flag is set to 0
1 Indicates flag is set to 1
\- Indicates flag is unaffected

```
LD  SP, nn
LD  SP, (nn)
LD  SP, IX
LD  SP, IY
```

You can examine the stack of the Sinclair ZX80 and ZX81 by using the editing program, and looking in the last 30-40 bytes from the top of your memory.
"** Do not change the contents of the locations in the stack**"

Almost any change will cause your Sinclair to crash - the screen will go black and you wil have to turn the power on again. This is because the operating system places a lot of information it requires on the stack and changes will cause it to bomb.

For the same reason do not try to manipulate the position of the stack pointer unless you are sure of what you are doing.

<u>NOTE</u>:

In a well organised program the number of POPs and PUSHes should end up the same no matter which path the program follows. Any miscalculation may lead to funny results.

Note also that whenever a subroutine is called, the return address is pushed on to the stack. We can therefore use this to examine the address at which the USR subroutine is called by means of the following program:

ZX80 Version:

```
        POP HL      ; get address in HL
        PUSH HL     ; put it back on stack
        RET
```

ZX81 Version:

```
        POP BC      ; get address in BC
        PUSH BC     ; put it back on stack
        RET
```

TWO FISTED ARITHMETIC

One of the benefits of being able to have 16-bit capabilities on what is effectively an 8-bit processor is that we can use the 16-bits to specify addresses, or to perform calculations involving integer numbers up to about 64,000 (or in the range - 32,000 to +32,000 if negative numbers are to be permitted).

In this light it is easy to see why the original Sinclair ZX80 limited all numbers to integers and to the range - 32,000 to +32,000.

But even though we can perform some arithmetic with two hands, our title for this chapter gives a hint of what is to come - two handed arithmetic is a little clumsy compared to one-handed arithmetic. The range of options is just not there!

FAVOURED REGISTER PAIR:

In the same way that the "A" register is the favoured register in 8-bit arithmetic, so there is a favoured register pair in 16-bit arithmetic, and it is the "HL" register pair.

This favoritism is not quite so pronounced as in the 8-bit case, so we do not omit the name of the register pair.

ADDITION:

The additions are quite straightforward:

```
ADD  HL,BC
ADD  HL,DE
ADD  HL,HL
ADD  HL,SP
```

But that is it!

Note that it is not possible to add an absolute number to HL - e.g. "Add HL,nn" is not permitted. To perform that kind of calculation we need to:

```
LD  DE,nn
ADD HL,DE
```

When you consider that this now ties up four of the 8-bit registers out of a total of 7, you realise it's not something you want to do too often.

Note also that there is no addition between "HL" and the index registers. You will also remember that there is no load instruction which permits you to transfer the contents of IX or IY to BC or DE, so the only way to do such an additon would be like:

```
PUSH  IX
POP   DE
ADD   HL,DE
```

INSTRUCTIONS FOR
TWO HANDED ARITHMETIC

MNEMONIC	BYTES	TIME TAKEN	EFFECT ON FLAGS C	Z	PV	S	N	H
ADD HL, Reg Pair	1	11	#	-	-	-	0	?
ADD HL,SP	2	11	#	-	-	-	0	?
ADC HL, SP	2	15	#	#	#	#	0	?
ADD IX, BC or DE	2	15	#	-	-	-	0	?
ADD IX, 1X	2	15	#	-	-	-	0	?
ADD IX, SP	2	15	#	-	-	-	0	?
ADD IY, BC or DE	2	15	#	-	-	-	0	?
ADD IY, 1Y	2	15	#	-	-	-	0	?
ADD IY, SP	2	15	#	-	-	-	0	?
SBC HL, Reg Pair	2	15	#	#	#	#	1	?
SBC HL, SP	2	15	#	#	#	#	1	?

<u>FLAGS NOTATION:</u>

# Indicates flag is altered by operation
0 Indicates flag is set to 0
1 Indicates flag is set to 1
- Indicates flag is unaffected
? Indicates effect is not known

The one point of note is the "SP" register - the stack pointer.This is one of the very few operations where "SP" is treated like a register proper, but obviously you can't use it as a variable! Think of what would happen to all the pops and pushes if you varied the contents of "SP" at will.

EFFECT ON FLAGS:

16-bit arithmetic is where the carry flag really comes insto a field of its own, because as you can see from the table at the beginning of this chapter, the only other flag that is affected by the "ADD" instruction is the "subtraction" flag (and all we are saying is that the "ADD" instruction is not a subtraction!)

The carry flag will be set if there is an overflow from the high bit of "H"(- any overflow from "L" is automatically placed into "H" by the calculation).

ADD WITH CARRY:

Because of the limited nature of 16-bits, we are able to chain additions just as in the 8-bit case. The instruction "Add with Carry" - mnemonic "ADC" operates in a similar manner to "add" and with the same range of register pairs:

```
ADC  HL,BC
ADC  HL,DE
ADC  HL,HL
ADC  HL,SP
```

16-BIT SUBTRACTION:

16-bit subrtraction is also a very straightforward operation, but there is no subtraction without carry: if you are not sure of the status of the carry flag, be sure that your program includes a line to clear the carry flag before any subtraction operation.

```
SBC  HL,BC
SBC  HL,DE
```

```
SBC  HL,HL
SBC  HL,SP
```

(That last instruction has obvious application: set "HL" to the end of the memory used by your program, screen display and variables, subtract "SP", and the result <negative> will be the amount of free space. Can you write a simple program to do that? See the end of the chapter to confirm your solution).

EFFECT OF CARRY ARITHMETIC ON FLAGS:

You may have noticed that three other flags are affected by the "Add with Carry" and "Subtract with Carry" that were not affected by the simple 16-bit addition instructions.

These are the zero flag, the sign flag and overflow flag. Each of these is set according to the result of the operation.

INDEX REGISTER ARITHMETIC:

Index registers are totally limited to addition without carry!

Furthermore the range of registers that can be added to the index registers is extremely limited:

Adding the "BC" or "DE" register pair
Adding the index register to itself
Adding the stack pointer.

SOLUTION TO MEMORY LEFT EXERCISE:

The end of the memory space the program uses is defined by the contents of the E-line memory location. These are different for the ZX80 and ZX81:

```
ZX80    E-line is in 16394,16395
ZX81    E-line is in 16404,16405
```

Obviously if we load HL with the contents of that location we are halfway there:

```
LD  HL,(E-line)
```

then subtract the "stack pointer":

```
SBC HL,SP
```

Because of the "carry" we need to clear the carry flag. This is most easily achieved by the "AND A" instruction, which is covered later in the book. Three-quarter marks if you knew you had to allow for the carry but didn't know how to do it. One-quarter marks if you forgot all about the carry.

Because the stack pointer is in higher memory than the top of your program (or else you are in diabolical trouble) the result will be negative.

Let us now proceed to get the number of bytes left as a positive number, using the "BC" register ("DE" would be just as good for this). We first want to shift HL to BC, but there is no "load" instruction to do this and we will need to use a push followed by a pop:

```
PUSH HL
POP BC
```

HL still has the same information as before, so HL=BC.

To get HL=-BC, subtract BC from HL twice (but don't forget that the carry has just been set by the subtraction so must be cleared again):

```
AND  A
SBC  HL,BC
SBC  HL,BC
```

HL now contains the negative value of what it contained before - i.e. the positive number of bytes left.

ZX81 users will now need to get the number into the "BC" register pair again to get a result from the "USR" function. To get "HL" back into "BC":

```
PUSH HL
POP  BC
```

and finally a return from the USR function:

```
RET
```

Did you get this right?

INSTRUCTIONS FOR LOGICAL OPERATORS

MNEMONIC	BYTES	TIME TAKEN	C	Z	PV	S	N	H
			EFFECT ON FLAGS					
AND register	1	4	0	#	#	#	0	0
AND number	2	7	0	#	#	#	0	0
AND (HL)	1	7	0	#	#	#	0	0
AND (IX + D)	3	19	0	#	#	#	0	0
AND (IY + D)	3	19	0	#	#	#	0	0
OR register	1	4	0	#	#	#	0	0
OR number	2	7	0	#	#	#	0	0
OR (HL)	1	7	0	#	#	#	0	0
OR (IX + D)	3	19	0	#	#	#	0	0
OR (IY + D)	3	19	0	#	#	#	0	0
XOR Register	1	4	0	#	#	#	0	0
XOR Number	2	7	0	#	#	#	0	0
XOR (HL)	1	7	0	#	#	#	0	0
XOR (IX + D)	3	19	0	#	#	#	0	0
XOR (IY + D)	3	19	0	#	#	#	0	0

FLAGS NOTATION:

# Indicates flag is altered by operation
0 Indicates flag is set to 0
1 Indicates flag is set to 1
- Indicates flag is unaffected.

LOGICAL OPERATORS

There are three operations which are as valuable in the field of machine (or assembly) language programming as the more commonly used "+", "-", multiplication or division. These are generally referred to as boolean operators after the man who formulated the rules of these operations. These operations are:

AND
OR
XOR

We are already familiar with the concept of operations which apply to an entire number, but the reason that these operations are so valuable is they operate on the individual bits of the number.

Let us look at one of these operations, "And":

BIT A	BIT B	RESULT BIT A "AND" BIT B
0	0	0
1	0	0
0	1	0
1	1	1

It is obvious that the result of an "AND"operation is to give us a "1" only if A AND B both contained a "1".

You may be asking yourself - "What is the point of such an operation?"

The "And" operation is extremely useful in that it allows us to mask a byte so that it is altered to contain only certain bits:

If for example, we wish to limit a particular variable to the range of 0 - 7 only, we quite clearly wish to indicate that we want only the bits 0 - 2 to contain information. (If bit 3 contained information, the number would be at least 8).

```
E.g.    0 0 0 0  0 1 0 1      = 5
        <------------>
        These bits
        must be "0".
```

If we therefore take a number whose value we do not know and apply the "and" operation with "7", the result will be a number which lies in tne range 0 - 7.

```
     E.g.          0 1 1 0  1 0 0 1      =105
                   0 0 0 0  0 1 1 1      =7 => Mask
                   ----------------------
Result of and      0 0 0 0  0 0 0 1      =1 => In
                                         range 0 - 7
```

Note that the Z80 chip only allows for the "AND" operation to take place with the "A" register. "A" can be "AND"ed with a value, any of the other 8-bit registers or with (HL).

```
E.g.      AND 7          Note that as only the "A"
          AND E          register can be acted on,
          AND (HL)       it need not be mentioned
                         in the instruction.
```

The same is true for the other Boolean operations, "OR" and "XOR".

The "OR" operation is very similar in concept to the "AND" operation:

BIT A	BIT B	BIT A "OR" BIT B
0	0	0
0	1	1
1	0	1
1	1	1

It is obvious that the result of an "OR" operation is to give us a "1" if either A or B contained a "1".

Again you may be asking what is the point of such an operation.
The "OR" operation is also extremely useful in that it allows us to set any bits in a number: if, for example, we wished to ensure that a number was odd, then quite clearly we have to set bit 0. (The same result could be obtained by using the "SET" instruction).

```
          LD  A,number
          OR  1              ;make number odd
```

The above two lines would be a typical mnemonic listing.

The concept of "XOR" - pronounced "Exclusive or" - is also easy to understand but its actual use in programming is more limited.
The result of "XOR" is a "1" only if one of A or B contains a "1".
In other words, the result is the same as for the "or" operation in all cases except when both A and B contain a "1".

XOR => OR - AND

BIT A	BIT B	BIT A "XOR" BIT B
0	0	0
1	0	1
0	1	1
1	1	0

The last thing we must consider is the effect that these operations have on the flags.

ZERO FLAG	This flag will be on (=1) if the result is zero
SIGN FLAG	This flag will be on (=1) if bit 7 of result is set
CARRY FLAG	Flag will be off (=0) after "AND", "OR", "XOR" i.e carry will be reset.
PARITY FLAG (Note that this flag also doubles as Overflow Flag)	This flag will be on (=1) if there is even no. of bits in the result: 0 1 1 0 1 1 1 0 => off 0 1 1 0 1 0 1 0 => on.
HALF-CARRY FLAG)) SUBTRACT FLAG)	Both flags turn off (=0) after "AND", "OR", "XOR" These flags are used in "BCD" arithmetic.

USE OF BOOLEAN OPERATIONS ON FLAGS:

There is a special case of the Boolean operators which is very handy - the case of the register A operating on itself.

AND A	A is unchanged, carry flag cleared
OR A	A is unchanged, carry flag cleared
XOR A	A is set to 0, carry flag cleared.

These instructions are often popular because they require only one byte to do what might otherwise require two. (Such as LD A,0).

The carry flag often needs to be cleared - e.g. as a matter of routine before using any of the arithmetic operations such as

ADC	Add with carry
SBC	Subtract with carry.

LOOPS AND JUMPS

Loops and Jumps is what gives a computer program real power. Once you have the ability to make decisions and to execute different bits of the programs as a result of previous calculations you are really getting places.

This freedom can also cause problems, create programs which are difficult to follow, and almost impossible to debug.

I would strongly suggest that you designed your computer programs carefully before entering code, and that is why we have included the chapter "Planning your Machine Language Program". I emphasise this now because loops and jumps are what will entice you away from good program design.

MACHINE LANGUAGE EQUIVALENT OF ˊGOTOˊ:

In BASIC, you are familiar with the instruction ˊGOTOˊ, which transfers control of your program to the instructions in the line you ˊGOTOˊ.

Nothing could be simpler to implement in machine language: just specify the memory location you would like to CPU to find the next instructions and you are half-way there.

The most simple instruction is "Jump To":

```
JP  XX XX
JP  (HL)
JP  (IX)
JP  (IY)
```

one of these instructions can also be made to be dependent on the status of one of the flags, such as the carry flag. This conditional Jump instrtuction is:

```
JP  CC,  NN
```

where CC is the condition to be met. If we had

JP Z,0000

for example, this would be read "Jump" if zero flag is set to address ´0000´. (This is the address the Sinclair jumps to when you turn the power on, and as such a ´JP´ to zero might be used in a machine language program if you wanted to clear all the memory and start again with ´K´).

Now note that the CPU does not allow for any mistakes. If you say ´Jump´, it will jump. Because almost any code can be construed as an instruction, the CPU does not care if you land it in the middle of data, or in the second byte of a two-byte instruction: it will read the byte at the address it finds and presumes that is the start of the next instruction.

The way the CPU works out the ´Jump´ instructions is really quite simple: it has a little counter called the "Program Counter" which tells it where to find the next instruction to be executed. In the normal course of programming (that is, without jumps) the CPU looks at the instruction to be executed and adds however many bytes there are to the instruction to the program counter.

Thus if it meets a 2-byte instruction, it adds 2, while a 4-byte instruction will make it add 4 to the program counter.

When it comes across a "Jump" instruction, it merely replaces the contents of the program counter with whatever value you have specified. That is why you cannot allow any errors to creep in.

LONG JUMPS AND SHORT JUMPS:

We can describe the above instructions to be the machine language equivalent of a ´Long Jump´ because the 16-bit address allows us to jump to anywhere the Z80 chip can possibly go.

The disadvantage of the long jump is that:

A. Often we don´t want to jump that far
   but still have to use a 3-byte instruction.

B. We cannot easily relocate the program to another part of memory because we are specifying the absolute address.

It was mainly to overcome these two disadvantages that the "Short Jump" was introduced. This is referred to as a "Relative Jump" and allows us to jump up to +127 bytes from our present position or up to -128 bytes from the present position. i.e. the distance jumped can be specified in one byte!

<u>RELATIVE JUMP INSTRUCTION</u>:

The instruction mode is simple:

```
        JR  d
```

where d is the relative displacement. We can also make the relative jump dependent on some condition, such as whether the carry is set, or the zero flag is set, for example, these conditional jumps are written as

```
        JR  cc, d
```

where cc is the condition to be met.

The value of the displacement is added to the "Program Counter".

This means it takes the present value of the program counter and adds the relative value you have specified. The value you specify can be either positive - jumping forward - or negative - jumping backwards! If you check back to our chapter on negative jumps you will realise this means that relative jumps are limited to the range -128 to +127.

Note that, when the CPU is executing a relative jump instruction, the program counter is already pointing to the next instruction which would be executed if the condition was not met.

This is because when the CPU comes across "JR" it knows that it has a 2-byte instruction to deal with and adds 2 to the program counter - the program counter is therefore pointing to the instruction after the relative jump!

E.g. In a program such as

LOCATION		CODE
17100		Add A,B
17101		JR Z,02H
17103		LD B,0
17105	Next	LD HL,4000H

The following is the way the CPU deals with the program:

Load byte at 171000
Byte is part of 1-byte instruction
so set program counter to 17101
Execute instruction

Load byte at 17101
Byte is part of 2-byte instruction
so set program counter to 17103
Get next byte to complete instruction
Execute instruction

Load byte at 17103
Byte is part of 2-byte instruction
so set program counter to 17105
Get next byte to complete instruction
Execute instruction

Now this is the part where the relative jump instruction has to decide what to do about the program counter:

If the zero flag is set, add 2 to the
program counter => 17105
If the zero flag is not set, do nothing
(program counter = 17103)

This also explains why there are two times shown for the time taken for this instruction. It takes less time to do nothing than to calculate the new program counter.

The CPU will therefore execute either the instruction at 17103 or the instruction at 17105 depending on the zero flag.

It is also possible to make the relative jump negative as we have already mentioned.

EXERCISE:

Because the relative jump is a 2-byte instruction, and the program counter is pointing to the next instruction after the relative jump, what would be the effect of an instruction which read:

```
JR  -2
```

MACHINE LANGUAGE "FOR ...NEXT" LOOPS:

You are, I am sure, familiar with the ´BASIC´ form of the "FOR ...NEXT" loop:

```
FOR I=1 to 6
LET C = C+1
NEXT I
```

The machine language equivalent is similar but takes a different form. Let us consider how we could implement the machine language loop using the arithmetic functions and the relative jump:

```
         LD B,1              ; Set Counter to 1
         LD A,7              ; Max. of Counter + 1
Loop     INC  C              ; C = C + 1
         INC B               ; Increment Counter
         CP B                ; is B=A?
         JR   NZ,Loop        ; if not loop again
```

This will work, but note the following: We are tying up 2 registers, one to increase, and one to hold the maximum; and the instruction which increments the counter does not set any flags on completion.

A much better way would be if we counted down!

We know that we have to do the loop 6 times, so why not set 'B' to 6 and count down?
This will give us:

```
         LD B,6              ; Set Counter
Loop     INC C               ; C = C + 1
         DEC B               ; Decrease Counter
         JR NZ,Loop          ; Loop if not finished
```

You can see that this is a much more efficient way of doing things.

The ZX80 chip has a special instruction which combines the last two lines above.

This instruction is written as:

```
         DJNZ  d
```

And is read as "Decrease (B) and Jump if Not Zero". (The d is the relative displacement). This instruction is a 2-Byte instruction and therefore saves one byte on the above coding.

Because of the existence of this special instruction, the 'B' register is usually used as a counting register.

The limitation of 'DJNZ' instruction is that one can only count up to 256.

DJNZ instructions can however be nested, if required:

```
         LD B,10H          ; B=16
Bigloop  PUSH BC           ; Save Value of "B"
         LD B,0            ; Set B=256
Litloop  ---
                           ; Whatever calculation
         ---
         DJNZ Litloop      ; Done 256 Times?
         POP BC            ; Get back value of B
         DJNZ Bigloop      ; Do Bigloop 16 times
```

Naturally the DJNZ instruction does not have to be used: You could just as easily code this by setting "BC" to 1000H, and used a short routine which decreased BC and tested it for zero.

<u>Waiting Loops:</u>

There are times in machine language programs when things happen so fast it is necessary to just wait a little while. Examples that spring to mind are sending information to a cassette (the pips have to be spaced sufficiently far apart to be able to read them later) or sending information to a typewriter (imagine printing thousands of characters a second!).

It is therefore useful to set up waiting loops using the DJNZ instructions:

```
         LD B,  Count
Wait     DJNZ   Wait
```

The instruction "DJNZ Wait" will cause the CPU to jump back to the DJNZ instruction as many times as required to set "B" back to zero before proceeding again.

This should give you the answer to our exercise of what happens when you write:

```
Wait     JR     Wait
```

You might be waiting quite a while for the CPU to exit this loop!

INSTRUCTIONS FOR CALL AND RETURN GROUP

MNEMONIC	BYTES	TIME TAKEN	C	Z	PV	S	N	H
CALL Address	3	17	-	-	-	-	-	-
CALL cc,Address	3	10/17	-	-	-	-	-	-
RET	1	10	-	-	-	-	-	-
RET cc	1	5/11	-	-	-	-	-	-

(EFFECT ON FLAGS: C, Z, PV, S, N, H)

Note: cc is condition to be met for instruction to be executed. The following are the conditions which can be used:

FLAG	ABBREVIATION	MEANING
CARRY	C	Carry Set (=1)
	NC	Carry Clear (=0)
Zero	Z	Zero Set (=1)
	NZ	Zero Clear (=0)
Parity	PE	Parity even (=1)
	PO	Parity odd (=0)
Sign	M	Sign Neg. (=1)
	P	Sign Pos. (=0)

FLAGS EFFECTED:
Note that none of the flags are effected by the call or return instructions.

TIMING:
Where two times are shown, the shorter time indicated is for the case of the condition not being met.

USE OF SUBROUTINES IN YOUR MACHINE LANGUAGE PROGRAMS

The use of subroutines is as easy in machine language programming as it is in ordinary basic programs, if not easier.

In fact, remember that using the "USR" function in your basic program is really calling a subroutine: we need to have a 'return' instruction to finish!

Therefore it is very easy for you to test certain subroutines independently of your main machine language program.

THE MAJOR DIFFERENCE THAT YOU WILL FACE IN IMPLEMENTING SUBROUTINES IN YOUR MACHINE LANGUAGE PROGRAM IS THAT IS IS NECESSARRY FOR YOU TO KNOW THE ADDRESS WHERE THE SUBROUTINE STARTS.

This can cause a problem if you store the machine language routines in a variable array, because the address of this variable is not necessarily fixed. See the last chapter on hints for storing programs which suggests that programs be stored in an array (so that they can be saved and reloaded) but moved to other addresses for execution.

Note that subroutines can also be called conditionally.

This is the machine language equivalent of the basic statement:

```
IF (condition) then GOSUB (address)
```

The difference is that the only conditions allowed are the status of four of the flags:

Carry flag
Zero flag
Parity flag (also overflow flag)
Sign flag

Remember that all these flags are set according to the last instruction which affected that particular flag.

It is therefore good practice to have "CALL" or "RETURN" instruction immediately after the instruction which sets the flag.

E.g.

```
        LD      A,(number)
        CP      1
        CALL    Z,one
        CP      2
        CALL    Z,two
        CP      3
        CALL    Z,three
```

The above routine allows you to jump to various routines depending on the value stored in the location "number".

A shorter routine is possible if you know that there are only the above three possibilities for the value stored in "number":

```
        LD      A,(number)
        CP      2
        CALL    Z,two       ; A = 2
        CALL    C,one       ; A < 2 => A = 1
        CALL    three       ; A > 2 => A = 3
```

This is because the instruction "CP 2" sets both the zero and carry flags and the call instructions do not affect any flags.

Similarly the use of the conditional return from a subroutine is very useful.

BLOCK OPERATIONS

You should by now be very familiar with the language your computer understands - it˝s very much like learning a foreign language: when you can think in that language you know you have mastered it.

This chapter covers the last set of very useful instructions - the next four chapters deal with instructions that are nice to have around and in some circumstances come into their own, but in general terms you should be able to write machine language programs with what you already know.

Be sure however to read the chapter on planning your machine language program!

The instructions covered in this chapter are by their very nature able to leap tall buildings in a single bound, faster than a speeding bullet - in other words, instructions which can operate on a block of memory rather than just single 8-bit bytes.

Let˝s start with the simplest of these:

CPI

With your knowledge of the Z80 Language, you should be able to immediately recognise this is a member of the "compare" family, and it is in fact an extended compare.

It is read in english as "compare and increase"- (you will remember that one can only compare with anything with the contents of Register ˝A˝, and this does not need to mentioned in the instruction.)

"CPI" compares ˝A˝ with (HL) and increases HL automatically. This means that after the CPI operation, HL is already pointing to the next location ready for a repeat.

With such an instruction we might be able to

INSTRUCTIONS FOR BLOCK COMPARE AND MOVE GROUP

MNEMONIC	BYTES	TIME TAKEN	C	Z	PV	S	N	H
			EFFECT ON FLAGS					
LDI	2	16	-	-	#	-	0	0
LDD	2	16	-	-	#	-	0	0
LDIR	2	21/16	-	-	0	-	0	0
LDDR	2	21/16	-	-	0	-	0	0
CPI	2	16	-	#	#	#	1	#
CPD	2	16	-	#	#	#	1	#
CPIR	2	21/16	-	#	#	#	1	#
CPDR	2	21/16	-	#	#	#	1	#

FLAGS NOTATION:

\# Indicates flag is altered by operation
0 Indicates flag is set to 0
1 Indicates flag is set to 1
\- Indicates flag is unaffected

TIMING:

For repeat instructions, the times shown are for each cycle. The shorter time indicated is for the case of the instruction terminating - eg. for CPIR, either BC = 0 or A = (HL).

Write a routine to search all of memory for a particular match, as follows:

```
Search          CPI
                 JR   NZ,  Search
```

In this way, unless a match is found (zero flag will be set as in all compare instructions) the program will keep on looking.

Unfortunately this is not such a good idea as unless a match is found the program would never end!

Fortunately the designers of the Z80 language thought of this and the CPI instruction also automatically decreases BC!

We can therefore select at will the length of the block we wish to search through and thus specify an end to the search.

Let's assume that the length of the block we are searching through is less than 256 bytes long, so that the BC count would only be stored in the C register, we could write:

```
Search          CPI
                 JR  Z, FOUND
                INC   C
                DEC   C
                JR   NZ, SEARCH
NOTFOUND        ---
FOUND           ---
```

Obviously a different routine would be implemented if the length of the block was more than 255 bytes. Note the use of the INC and DEC instructions to test whether C = 0. These two instructions only require one byte each, and as they both affect the zero flag the net effect is to set the flag only if C was originally zero. The other benefit is that coding does not alter any of the other registers.

Now we could also wish to search a block of memory starting from the top rather than from the bottom, and we therefore have the instruction:

CPD

Which is read in english as "compare and decrease". The decrease refers to HL of course, and the effect on BC is still the same!

Even more powerful than these two instructions are the real supermen:

CPIR
CPDR

These are read as "Compare, Increase and Repeat"
and "Compare, Decrease and Repeat".

These 2-byte instructions are unbelievably powerful: they allow the CPU to automatially continue searching through the block of memory until either a match is found or the end of block is reached. (Naturally we have to specify A, HL and BC before starting, but even so this is unbelievably economical coding).

Because the instruction will stop for one of two possibilities (ie. match found in middle of block or no match found at all) we have to ensure we use some code at the end to differentiate between the two possibilities.

*** *** ***

Users who are going to be writing machine code for the ZX81 and who wish to also make facility of the "SLOW" mode to enable continuous display should be very careful in using CPIR and other similar instructions as they can be very time consuming instructions.

CPIR, for example, requires 21 cycles for each byte to be searched. Admittedly there are 4,000,000 cycles in each second, but even so this means that searching through 4,000 bytes requires 1/50th of a second.

This may not seem like a very long time to you but when you remember that the interrupt will also come every 1/50th of a second or so to display the screen the net effect is to cause a flicker in the screen. (This is because the interrupt cannot stop an instruction in the middle).

Experience has shown that instructions which take as little as 100 cycles (ie. searching through a block of 5 bytes!) can cause flickering, but of course only if the interrupt comes during execution of that instruction. You may have to weigh up the disadvantages of flicker against the possibility of that instruction being processed when the interrupt comes.

Typically the ZX81 in SLOW mode will process the program for about 1400 cycles before being interrupted. Thus an instruction with a time of a 100 cycles has a 7% chance of being executed when the interrupt comes.

***   ***   ***

The remaining block operations are along the lines of "move it, mate".

These are:

```
LDI          LDIR
LDD          LDDR
```

Obviously part of the "Load" family these are read as:

LOAD AND INCREASE
LOAD, INCREASE AND REPEAT
LOAD AND DECREASE
LOAD, DECREASE, AND REPEAT

Taking the simplest one first, ´LDI´ is really a combination of the following set of actions:

LOAD (DE) WITH (HL)
INCREMENT DE, HL
DECREMENT BC

Note that this is the only instruction that will load from one memory location to another without having to be loaded into a register first.

The use of the ´DE´ register as the destination address is very clever - this way you never forget which register holds the DE-STINATION!

The symmetrical instruction "LDD" is exactly the same except that HL and DE are decreased as loading proceeds. The difference between "LDI" and "LDD" is more important when the two blocks (the one where the information is and the one where the information is going) overlap.

Suppose we are using this instruction in a word processing application, and we want to delete a word from a sentence:

    The big brown dog jumped over the fox.

If we now want to delete the word "brown" all we need to do is to move the rest of the sentence to the left by 6 characters.

```
DE = DESTINATION = CHARACTER 9
HL = SOURCE      = CHARACTER 15
BC = COUNT       = 24 CHARACTERS.
```

Let us start with LDI: after one instruction we have

    The big drown dog jumped over the fox.

And HL= 10, DE= 16, BC= 23.

After 2 more instructions:

    The big dogwn dog jumped over the fox.

And after all the instructions have been completed:

    The big dog jumped over the fox.e fox.

(If we had wanted the portion after the full stop to be blanked out this could have been achieved by adding blanks at the end of the original sentence and increasing BC to say 30.)

If we now want to reverse the process and return the word "brown" to the sentence, we can't simply use "LDI" again because we will overwrite the information we want to shift:

```
EG.  HL = SOURCE        = CHARACTER 9
     DE = DESTINATION   = CHARACTER 15
     BC = COUNT         = 24 CHARACTERS.
```

After one instruction we would have:

    The big dog judped over the fox.e fox.

After 6 instructions we would have:

    The big dog judog juver the fox.e.fox.

So far so good. But another three gives:
    The big dog judog jud og the fox.e.fox.

The problem is that we have overwritten the information we want to transfer.

We therefore have to use the 'LDI' instruction, with the DE register pointing to the end of the sentence.

The instructions 'LDIR' and 'LDDR' are even more powerful, able to shift thousands of bytes around very quickly.

EXERCISE:

Write a short routine to transer 32 bytes from the ROM part of memory to the screen.
Be sure to define a line full of blanks in the basic program before calling the USR function.
ZX80 users could try moving 32 bytes from location 0BC0H.
ZX81 users could try moving 32 bytes from location 0190H.

Z80 INSTRUCTIONS THAT

ARE LESS FREQUENTLY USED

REGISTER EXCHANGES

We briefly discussed in the first few chapters the idea of the CPU having gloves it could put on or take off, and thus store some information in a place that is more accessible than memory locations.

You must remember that you cannot manipulate these alternate registers and the analogy with gloves is a very valuable one. While they will retain their shape, there is no way they can do any arithmetic or counting by themselves.

The first instruction is:

```
     EX AF,AF'
```

This does exactly what its name suggests: "Exchange the register pair AF and AF´". In the gloves analogy we would say "Swap gloves on the pair of hands AF".

ZX81 users should be extememly cautious about using this instruction. The manual states that the AF alternate register pair is used by the display routine and using the "EX AF, AF´" instruction may cause the program to crash. (This is because if the screen refresh comes when you have the wrong set of gloves on, the program will look for the information to be displayed in the wrong place).

The next general swap gloves instruction is:

```
   EXX
```

This instruction swaps the gloves on all other 8-bit registers as follows:

```
            B  C           B´  C´
            D  E    <=>    D´  E´
            H  L           H´  L´
```

This is therefore a very powerful instruction but its very power makes it limited in use. This is because it acts on all the registers at once and it is not possible to hold any value back. (Except in register ´A´ which is not affected by "EXX").

The only way around this problem is to write a short routine along the lines of:

```
        PUSH    HL
        EXX
        POP     HL
```

This means that you have saved the values of BC,DE and HL in the alternate set of registers but still have HL´s value to work with.

The last instruction in this group does not really fall within the swap gloves type:

```
        EX      DE,HL
```

In this instruction DE gets the contents of HL and HL the contents of DE.

This instruction is indeed very useful, because as we saw HL is a favoured register pair in many applications and there are times when the value we want to manipulate is in DE.

BIT, SET AND RESET

So far all the instructions we have been dealing with have involved the manipulation of 8-bit or 16-bit numbers.

The "Bit, Set and Reset" group allows us to manipulate the single bits of registers of contents of memory locations. Because of the very tedious nature of fiddling with single bits this is not a very commonly used group of instructions.

Furthermore, it tends to take even longer to set a single bit in a register or memory location than it does to change or examine the entire 8 bits of that memory location or register.

Nonetheless there are times when you need to know whether a bit in the middle is set or not, or even to set a bit. Note however that many of the bit setting or resetting can be carried out using the logical operators.

The "Bit, Set and Reset" group of instructions allows us to turn any bit "on" or "off" at will, or even just look at a specified bit to see what its status is.

Let us look at the first set of instructions:

```
SET  n, r
SET  n, (HL)
SET  n, (IX+d)
SET  n, (IY+d)
```

The "SET" instruction turns "On" (i.e. = 1) the bit numbered ´n´ (using the notation 0 - 7) in register ´r´ or in the specified memory location.

No changes are made to any of the flags.

The "RESET" group of instructions operate on exactly the same range of registers or memory locations, but instead of turning the bits "On", it turns the bits "Off" (i.e. = 0).

The "BIT" instructions should really be read as "BIT?" in English as the function of this instruction is to test the contents of the indicated bit.

No changes are made to the registers or memory locations but the zero flag is altered according to the status of the bit tested.

```
If Bit = 0    then   zero flag is set on ( =1 )
If Bit = 1    then   zero flag is set off( =0 )
```

This may seem confusing at first glance but think of it this way: if the bit is zero, then the zero flag is raised; if the bit is on, then naturally the zero flag would not be raised.

ROTATE AND SHIFTS

You can move them to the left, you can move them to the right, you can shift those registers any which way you like.

The trick is to differentiate between the various shifts and rotate in order to know which one to use when and to remember that the ˊCarryˊ bit can often be considered to be a 9th bit of the registers. (I.e. the Carry is bit # 8 if the bits are numbered 0 - 7).

Some rotate instructions go right through the Carry (as the 9th bit) so that the entire rotation goes through a cycle of 9 bits. For example, let us look at ˊRLAˊ (the meaning of each instruction will be made clear later in this chapter):

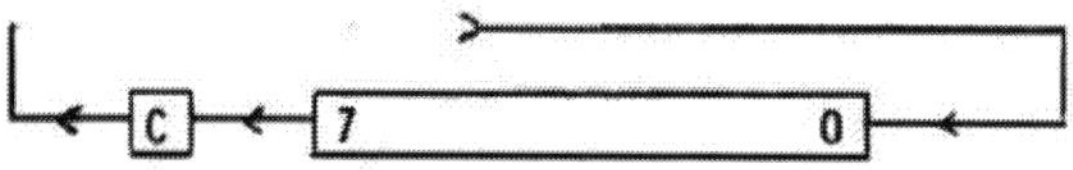

Other rotations involve only an 8-bit cycle, although the carry flag is changed according to the bit which has to go the ˊLong way roundˊ. An example of this is the ˊRLCAˊ instruction:

This means that in a left rotation as above the contents of bit 0 are transferred to bit 1, bit 1 to 2, etc., but the contents of bit 7 are transferred to both the carry bit and to bit 0. Compare this with the ˊRLAˊ instruction above where bit 7 gets transferred to the carry bit and the carry bit gets transferred to bit 0.

LEFT ROTATIONS:

There are basically two types of left rotations:

* ROTATE LEFT REGISTERS - this is a 9-bit cycle rotation as illustrated above for ´RLA´

RLA - "Rotate left accumulator"
RL r - "Rotate left register r"

* ROTATE LEFT CIRCULAR - the ´Circular´ means that the cycle is only 8-bits as with the RLCA instruction illustrated above.

RLCA	- Rotate left circular ´A´
RLC r	- Rotate left circular ´r´
RLC (HL)	- Rotate left circular (HL)
RLC (IX+d)	- Rotate left circular (IX+d)
RLC (IY+D)	- Rotate left circular (IY+d)

As well as these two left rotate instructions there is a SHIFT LEFT instruction available, but this can only operate on register 'A':

SLA - shift left accumulator

This is different in that the contents of the carry bit are lost and bit zero is filled with 0. This is effectively multiplying 'A' by 2 as long as nothing is transferred to the accumulator. (Think about 'SLA' if A = 80H).

<u>RIGHT ROTATIONS:</u>

Once again we have the two basic modes of rotations but this time to the right. Exactly the same range of possible memory locations and rotations can be spinned to the right as to the left.

RRA - Rotate right accumulator
RR r - Rotate right register

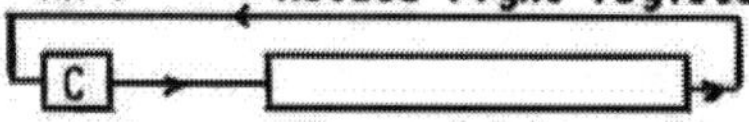

RRCA - Rotate right circular 'A'
RRC r - Rotate right circular 'r'
RRC (HL) - Rotate right circular (HL)
RRC (IX+d) - Rotate right circular (IX+d)
RRC (IY+d) - Rotate right circular (IY+d)

A similar shift right is available as for shift left:

SRL r - Shift right logical register 'r'

In this case this is pure division by 2 as long as we are using unsigned numbers (i.e the number range we wish to represent is 0 - 255).

Because in some applications we use the convention to indicate negative numbers by setting bit 7 to 1 (i.e giving us a range of -128 to +127) there is an addition shift right instruction called

SRA r - Shift right arithmetic "r"

As you can see this is also a division by 2 but it preserves the sign bit.

IN AND OUT:

In and Out is just about as simple a concept as you could get in machine language programming.

There are times when the CPU needs to get information from the outside world ("No CPU is an island?"), such as from the keyboard or from the cassette player.

As far as the CPU is concerned that´s totally foreign territory and as all good CPUs it will never leave home. The most it is prepared to do is to open a door to allow deliveries. The CPU doesn´t know and doesn´t care to know how a cassette player works.

All the relevent information is which door the cassette man is going to be delivering his goodies to - there is a choice of up to 256 doors for the Z80 chip but the actual number available to a particular CPU is a result of decisions made by the hardware manufacturers. As far as the Sinclair is concerned there is only the keyboard, the printer and the cassette player.

The other thing the CPU doesn´t want to know about is how the data is being transmitted. As far as it´s concerned, if it´s coming in or going out, it´s an 8-bit byte.

The keyboard is on the other side of door FE, so that to get data in from the keyboard you use the instruction

```
IN  A,(FE)
```

Now you may be asking yourselves how the 40 keys of the keyboard are arranged so as to be represented by 8-bit bytes.

The answer is not what you would expect - the keyboard only returns information from 5 keys at a time. It is the value of ´A´ as the door is opened which determines which set of 5 keys are going to be examined!

The keyboard is divided into 4 rows, each comprising two blocks of 5 keys:

```
3 => ( 1   2 3 4 5 )    ( 6 7 8 9 0   ) <= 4
2 => ( Q   W E R T )    ( Y U I O P   ) <= 5
1 => ( A   S D F G )    ( H J K L N/L ) <= 6
0 => ( SFT Z X C V )    ( B N M . SPC ) <= 7
```

You can see that there are 8 blocks of letters and we should therefore be able to correlate this with the 8 bits of "A". This is in fact the case:

All of the bits of "A" are set to "ON" except for one bit which specifies the block to be read.

You can think of it as something like a secret handshake - as the CPU goes to the door to get the information the handshake determines which piece of information it gets.

Thus to read the keys in the block " 1 2 3 4 5 ", it is bit 3 of "A" which should be off:

A = 1 1 1 1 0 1 1 1 = F7

The contents of the keyboard are returned in "A" with the information coming into the lower bits of "A":

i.e Key "1" -> bit 0 of "A"
Key "2" -> bit 1 of "A"

If block 4 was chosen instead (i.e A = EF) then the information would come in as:

Key "0" -> bit 0 of "A"
Key "9" -> bit 1 of "A"

You can think of the information coming into "A" from the outside edges first, so that both "0" and "1" would both go to bit "0" of register "A".

For some games applications you may wish to allow all of the top row to be read, and it it possible to read it all in one instruction (rather than the two instructions which would be required if we read one block at a time).

This is done by fooling the doorman into giving you two lots of information at once:
e.g.   A = 1 1 1 0 0 1 1 1 =E7
Note that both bits "3" and "4" are "off".

This handshake tells the doorman that the CPU wants the information from block 3 and block 4, and that is what it will get. Of course the two lots of information get jumbled and it is not possible for you to tell whether key "0" or key "1" was pressed, for example - both would set bit 0 of "A".

i.e.   "1" or "0" -> bit 0 of A
         "2" or "9" -> bit 1 of A
                  etc

This is useful in movement games because it enables keys "5" and "8" to be used as the left and right direction arrows even though they belong to different blocks in the keyboard.

Note that if you use the instruction

```
IN R, (C)
```

where register "C" specifies which door you want, then it is the contents of register "B" which define which keyboard block is being selected.

The other doors which will be of interest to those people trying to write a routine to enable them to load data or save data on cassette (it can be done) are obviously the cassette input/output doors.

These are doors "FF" for sending information to the cassette, and door "FE" for getting information in, but the major problem involved is the timing of the data going out and going in. This kind of problem requires a lot of experience with machine language programming and calculations of the time required for each instruction path.

PROGRAMMING

YOUR SINCLAIR

PLANNING YOUR MACHINE LANGUAGE PROGRAM

Machine language programming is extremely flexible in that it allows you to do anything at all.

Since all the higher level languages ultimately have to come down to machine language, it follows that anything you can program in Fortran or Cobol or any other language can be done in machine language.

With the additional benefit that the machine language program will be the faster one.

This total flexibility can however also be a trap to the unwary programmer. With so much freedom, it it possible to do anything. Unlike the Sinclair's basic operating system, for example, there are no checks on whether the statement is a legal one.

Since all numbers you can enter will be an instruction of one kind or another, the Z80 chip will process everything.

But even beyond the problems of checking whether the Syntax is legal, machine language programming has no constrains on your logic - you can perform functions, jumps, etc which would be totally illegal in any higher level language.

It is therefore of the utmost importance to discipline yourself in the design of machine language programming. I cannot recommend too highly the concept of the 'top-down' approach in programming in general, but especially in machine language programming.

The 'Top-down' approach forces you to break down the problem into smaller units, and enables you to check the logic of your design without doing any coding for a long time.

Suppose you wanted to write a lunar lander program:
The very first approach might be something along the lines

```
Instr           Display instruction
                Jump back to instr till n/line pressed
Draw            Draw landscape, start lander at top
Land            Move lander
                If fuel finished go to crash
                Jump back to land if not ground
Ground          Print congratulations
                Jump back to instr for next go
Crash           Print commiserations on bad landing
                Jump back to instr for next go
```

Notice how this "program" is written totally in English. At this stage, no decision has been made whether the program is to be written in BASIC or machine language. Nor is it necessary to make that decision - the concept of the lunar lander program is not dependent on the coding.

Now comes the part of logic testing.
You play the part of the computer and see if all the possibilities you wish to see included in the program are covered.

Are there any jumps to things you meant to write in but forgot? Is everything there? Are some routines redundent? Should some of the things be put into subroutines.

Let us look at the "program" again - oh, oh: we forgot to allow any way to finish the program!

The above logic might be fine for some applications, such as an arcade machine, but in your program you decide you would like to be able to turn the program off.

We now change the last part of the program as follows:

```
Ground                  Print congratulations
                        Jump to finish
Crash                   Print commiserations on bad landing
Finish                  Ask player if finished
```

If no, Jump to instr
If yes, stop

Note that we have used labels to describe certain lines in the program. These are very valuable, the more so if you choose short labels which are descriptive in their meaning.

Once this level is finished, you move one level down to do the same thing to one of the lines or modules above.
This is why this approach is called the Top Down approach.

For example, we can expand the ´finish´ module above:

```
Finish                  Clear screen
                        Print "Would you like to stop now?"
                        Scan keyboard for input
                        If input = yes then stop
                        Jump to instr
```

The other benefit of the top down approach is that you can test and run a particular module on its own, so that is is ready for the final program.

Let us go down one level further again, and look at the
Clear screen
line in more detail.

By this stage we do have to decide on what language we will write the program in, and let us choose machine language on the Sinclair.

If you were writing in BASIC, all you would have to say is : 900 CLS, but in machine language that simple sentence, ´Clear Screen´ can be deceptive (because of the way the Sinclair uses the screen display we must remember to fill in the end of lines!).

We might therefore do something like:

```
Clear                   Find screen beginning
                        Fill next 768 positions with blanks
                        Get screen beginning again
```

```
Fill that byte with "End-Line"
For lines 1 to 24
! Skip next 32 bytes
! Fill next byte with "End-Line"
Next line
```

We still haven't done any coding, but obviously the approach is based on machine language. The next level down is the one which does the coding, so let us look at filling the screen with blanks:

```
Clear   LD  HL, (Screen)          ;Screen start
        LD  BC, 768               ;Bytes to clear
        LD  D,0                   ;D = blank
Loop    LD  (HL),D                ;Fill blank
        INC HL                    ;Next position
        DEC BC                    ;Reduce count
        LD  A,B
        OR  C                     ;Test if BC = 0
        JR  NZ,Loop               ;Again if not end
```

Now you can deal with programs of such length quite easily and in this way build up very complex programs indeed.
By the way, you no doubt understand now why machine language programs tend to be so long and why people invented the higher language programs!

EXERCISES:

There are more ways than one to write any particular routines, so let us look at the simple clear screen routine written above.

This could be handled by several different approaches.

EXERCISE 1:

Can you think of a way that would enable the Loop to blank 768 positions without using the BC register, but using the B register only so that we may make use of the "DJNZ" instruction?

EXERCISE 2:

Can you think of a way that would enable the 768 positions to be blanked using the more powerful "LDIR" instruction?

Think carefully of what "LDIR" does: It is not always necessary to have 768 blank positions elsewhere!

ANSWERS:

More than one possible answer can be "right" - the only test is does it work?

USING DJNZ:

```
     CLEAR        LD  HL, (SCREEN)
                  LD  A,0
                  LD  B,A          ;SET B=256
                  LD (HL),A        ;
                  INC HL           ;FILL IN
                  LD (HL),A        ; 3 X 256
                  INC HL           ; BYTES
                  LD (HL),A
                  INC HL
                  DJNZ LOOP
```

USING LDIR:

```
     CLEAR        LD HL,(SCREEN) ;SOURCE
                  PUSH HL
                  POP DE
                  INC DE           ;DEST = HL+1
                  LD BC,768        ;HOW MANY
                  LD(HL),0         ;1ST POS = 0
                  LDIR             ;MOVE IT
```

If you add up the memory required, the first two methods each require 14 bytes and the last 13 bytes.

DEBUGGING AND EDITING

YOUR MACHINE LANGUAGE PROGRAM

The first issue for you to consider after you have designed your program and know what it is you want it to achieve is for you to decide where to put it in memory.

Sounds simple? Not really on the Sinclair ZX 80 or ZX 81. If your program is only a few lines long, then there may not be any problem. You can just enter it again using "Poke" commands, either manually or through a BASIC program just for that purpose.

In this case, all you need is to have spare "RAM" memory for your program:

```
1000 LET PROGRAMSTART = 17000
1010 FOR I = 0 TO PROGRAMLENGTH
1020 POKE PROGRAMSTART+I, DATA(I)
1030 NEXT I
```

The machine code values are stored in an array specially set aside for this purpose. Note that this is fine for a short program, but not very efficient because each machine code byte occupies one variable location: This is 2 bytes on the ZX80 and 5 bytes on the ZX81.

The following are the possible storage locations for machine language programs:

FREE RAM MEMORY
REM STATEMENT
PRINT STATEMENT
VARIABLE ARRAYS

Each of these has certain advantages and disadvantages, so let us examine each in turn.

A. FREE RAM MEMORY

This is OK for very short programs but the disadvantages are:

RAM MEMORY IS SET TO ZERO
BY "RUN" OR "GOTO" IN ZX81.
CANNOT BE SAVED ON TAPE>

These disadvantages make it almost impossible for programs of any length to be debugged or run from free RAM.

B. DIRECT CODE "POKED" INTO REM STATEMENT

Using this method, the actual code values are poked directly int the REM statement.
A line in the Basic program (usually the first one, so that its location in memory is known) is set up at the beginning with as many characters as expected in the machine language program.

```
EG.       100 REM AAAAAA ---- (128 A'S)
               ----AAAAAA
          110 ETC.
```

The actual contents of the REM statement is not important - you can use A, X, graphic characters or whatever.

ADVANTAGES:

STARTING ADDRESS IS KNOWN
(THIS IS VERY VALUABLE FOR SUBROUTINES)
CODE IS IN DIRECT FORM FOR RUNNING.

DISADVANTAGES:

DIFFICULT TO INSERT ADDITIONAL CODE.
SOME CHARACTERS ARE UNLISTABLE (OLD ROM
ONLY - CAUSES PROBLEMS.)
PROGRAM HANGS UP IF "118" IS POKED IN -
EG> CP 118.

Nonetheless this method offers many advantages, and is especially useful for storing subroutines which have already been debugged.

C. HEX CODE STORED IN REM STATEMENT OR IN PRINT STATEMENTS:

In this situation, the direct code is not stored but rather the hexidecimal representation.
EG.

```
         1120 REM CDA01 -- (AS MUCH CODE AS REQUIRED) --

OR       560  PRINT "CDA01 -- ETC --"
```

This means that you need to have part of your Basic program (or a special USR routine) devoted to translating the hexidecimal representation and then poking the codes into free memory or into arrays as required.

As many lines a necessary can be used. You might decide to have 16 instructions/basic line, or have each line contain a particular subroutine or module for easy manipulation.

ADVANTAGES:

'LISTING' CAN BE EASILY VIEWED
INSERTIONS AND DELETIONS ARE EASY

DISADVANTAGES:

PROGRAM CODE TAKES THREE TIMES AS MUCH ROOM AS CODE ONLY WOULD

SPECIAL LOADING ROUTINE REQUIRED.

USE OF LOADING ROUTINE REQUIRED WITH EVERY ALTERATION TO CODE.

Despite its advantages this is probably the best way to develop and debug long programs. Once they have been fully tested, the REM or PRINT statement is no longer required and the code can be stored as direct code in a REM statement or in an array.

D. DIRECT CODE STORED IN AN ARRAY

This is probably the best place to store your machine code program once it has been fully debugged and tested - except for subroutines!

An array is dimensioned as the first line of the "Basic" program:

```
100 DIM A(100)
```

In this way, the array is the first variable to be stored and its starting can be obtained by using the system variables.

The code is "Poked" into the array either by the "Basic" program or by you.

The main benefit stems from the fact that the code can then be easily "saved" on to tape and is ready to run. You also have the protection of other people not being to read your code easily.

ADVANTAGES:

VERY COMPACT MODE OF STORING
NO BASIC PROGRAMMING NEEDED
PROGRAMS CAN BE SAVED
NO PROBLEMS WITH SCREEN DISPLAY

DISADVANTAGES:

STARTING ADDRESS MUST BE COMPUTED
(MAKES SUBROUTINES IMPOSSIBLE)
DIFFICULT TO EDIT
LIMITED IN LENGTH TO MAX ARRAY

MAJOR POINTS TO WATCH OUT FOR:

One of the worst pitfalls in testing and debugging machine language programs comes from the relative jump instructions.

Although these instructions are very powerful and extremely useful, they do make life somewhat difficult whenever a change has to be made.

At all times check that your calculations of the relative jumps are correct before running a program - one wrong calculation and your computer will display the "Lost in Space" syndrome.

This means that when you are debugging a program, you must be especially careful not to insert or delete any instructions without first checking that these changes will not effect any relative jumps!

As it´s almost impossible to keep all these things in mind as you try to work out why the perfect program isn´t functioning, it is a good idea to follow the following rules:

```
          WHEN DELETING INSTRUCTIONS, REPLACE
              THE UNWANTED CODE BY ´NOP´ (=00).
          IF INSERTING CODE LONGER THAN ORIGINAL
              USE ´JP PATCH´ ( = C3 DD DD).
```

The ´NOP´ is a very valuable instruction that we did not deal with in any of the earlier chapters.

The ´NOP´ instruction means "NO OPERATION", and you can have as many of these as you like anywhere in your program without damage.

The code for "NO OPERATION" is so simple, you´ll never forget it - ZERO!

When your program is finished and working to your satisfaction, you can clean things up by deleting all these ´NOP´ -after working out the new relative jumps of course.

Inserting new code is more difficult, and involves patching. It cannot be recommended too highly for you to keep a notebook of editing you are making as you go along, so that when your program is working, you can bring back a semblance of order!

The "JP PATCH" instruction is three bytes long, so make sure any code you are replacing is included in the patch.

E.G.   Original Code =

```
17300      LD   B,56
           LD  HL,17312
```

But you decide that you really need to load BC not only B at location 17300.

The original instruction is 2 bytes, while

```
       LD    BC,56
```

is a three byte instruction.

Let us look at the actual memory location contents:

```
17300     06
17301     38        ;LD  B,56
17302     01
17303     A0
17304     43        ;LD  HL,17312
```

The solution is to put in the ´JP PATCH INSTRUCTION´ at 17302. because this then destroys the first byte of the "LD HL, 17312" instruction, we must now delete that instruction and include it in the patch.

The new listing will look like:

```
17300     JP      19000       ;JUMP TO PATCH

19000     LD      BC,56       ;CORRECT CODE
          LD      HL,17312
          JP      17303       ;RETURN TO MAIN
```

Let us look at the memory locations again:

```
17300     C3
17301     38
17302     4A
17303     00        ;NOP
17304     00        ;NOP

19000     01
19001     00
19002     38
   etc.
```

DISPLAYING 100 BYTES IN HEX

ZX 81 VERSION

```
100 PRINT "ENTER START"
110 INPUT S
120 LET S = INT (S/10)
130 CLS
140 FOR R = S TO S+9
150 PRINT "="; 10*R ; ">"
160 FOR I = 0 TO 9
170 LET V = PEEK (10*R+I)
180 LET H = INT (V/16)
190 LET L = V - 16*H
200 PRINT CHR$(H+28); CHR$(L+28); " ";
210 NEXT I
220 PRINT
230 NEXT R
240 PRINT
250 PRINT "NEXT 100?"
260 INPUT I$
270 LET S = S+10
280 IF CODE (I$) = 62 THEN GO TO 130
```

ZX 80 VERSION

Enter program as above, but alter lines 120 and 180 to read as follows:

```
120 LET S = S/10
180 LET H = V/16
```

MACHINE CODE EDITOR

ZX81 VERSION

```
100 PRINT "START?"
110 INPUT S
120 CLS
130 PRINT "MEMORY";TAB 10;"CODE"
140 FOR I = 0 TO 10
150 LET V = PEEK (S+I)
160 GO SUB 500
170 PRINT S+I; TAB 7; A$;
180 INPUT A$
190 IF A$ = "" THEN GO TO 220
200 LET V = 16 * CODE (A$) + CODE (A$(2)) - 476
210 POKE S+I, V
220 LET V = PEEK (S+I)
230 GO SUB 500
240 PRINT TAB 10; A$
250 IF V = 201 THEN GO TO 270
260 NEXT I
270 PRINT "CHANGES?";
280 INPUT A$
290 IF CODE (A$) = 62 THEN GO TO 120
300 PRINT "   MORE?"
310 INPUT A$
320 LET S = S + 10
330 IF CODE (A$) = 62 THEN GO TO 120
340 CLS
350 PRINT "START FOR USR?"
360 INPUT S
370 PRINT USR (S)
380 STOP
500 LET H = INT (V/16)
510 LET L = V - 16 * H
520 LET A$ = CHR$ (H+28) + CHR$ (L+28)
530 RETURN
```

NOTE: This program will fit into the standard 1K ZX81 machine and allow code to be entered in hexadecimal format into free memory, ˝REM˝ statements (e.g. Line 90 REM AAAAAAAAAAA), or into variables (e.g. Line 90 DIM A(4)).

This program will also ˝RUN˝ the machine language program if required. If you do not desire to ˝RUN˝ the program, reply "XX" to query "START FOR USR?"

MACHINE CODE EDITOR

ZX 80 VERSION

```
100 PRINT "START?"
110 INPUT S
120 CLS
130 PRINT "MEMORY","CODE"
140 FOR I = 0 TO 20
150 LET V = PEEK (S+I)
160 GO SUB 500
170 PRINT S+I, CHR$(H);CHR$(L);"  ";
180 INPUT A$
190 IF A$ = "" THEN GO TO 220
200 LET V = 16*CODE (A$) + CODE (TL$(A$) ) - 476
210 POKE S+I, V
220 LET V = PEEK (S+I)
230 GO SUB 500
240 PRINT CHR$(H);CHR$(L)
250 IF V = 201 THEN GO TO 270
260 NEXT I
270 PRINT "CHANGES?",
280 INPUT A$
290 IF CODE (A$) = 62 THEN GO TO 120
300 PRINT "MORE?"
310 INPUT A$
320 LET S = S+20
330 IF CODE (A$) = 62 THEN GO TO 120
340 CLS
350 PRINT "START FOR USR?"
360 INPUT S
370 PRINT USR (S)
380 STOP
500 LET H = V/16
510 LET L = V - 16*H + 28
520 LET H = H + 28
530 RETURN
```

Note: This program will fit into the standard 1K ZX80 Machine and allow code to be entered in hexadecimal format into free memory, "REM" statements (eg. line 90 REM AAAAAAAAAA), or into variables (eg. line 90 DIM A(10)).

This program will also "RUN" the machine language program if required. If you do not desire to "RUN" the program, reply "XX" to query "Start for USR?"

PROGRAM TO LOAD CODE

FROM REM LINE TO ARRAY

The following program is for the ZX81 with additional memory. (A modified version of this program can easily be written for the ZX80.) Use the "Machine Code Editor" program and add the following lines:

```
90  REM AAA -- at least 52 chars --- AAA
100 DIM A(100)
```

Add the following lines at the end of the program as dummy code:

```
1000  REM ABCD
1010  REM 1234
```

The aim of this program is to transfer the code in the REM lines starting at line 1000 into the Array "A". The REM lines can be any length; the only requirement is that code is entered in hexadecimal format - the program will crash if you do not have code as 2-digit pairs.

Now <RUN> the program and answer 16514 to the query "START?". 16514 is the location of the first usable character in the REM statement in line 90.

Enter code as overleaf, and when finished answer 16514 to query "Start for USR?". The 4 dummy codes should be transferred to the Array. To check on this, enter the following line without line number:

```
PRINT PEEK 16400 + 256 * PEEK 16401 <NEW LINE>
```

This will return the address of the start of Array "A". Enter <GOTO 100> <NEW LINE> and answer that address for "START"?.

Note: Do not use <RUN> or <GOTO 1> as this will redimension Array "A" and set all values to 0.

Contents of memory should be:

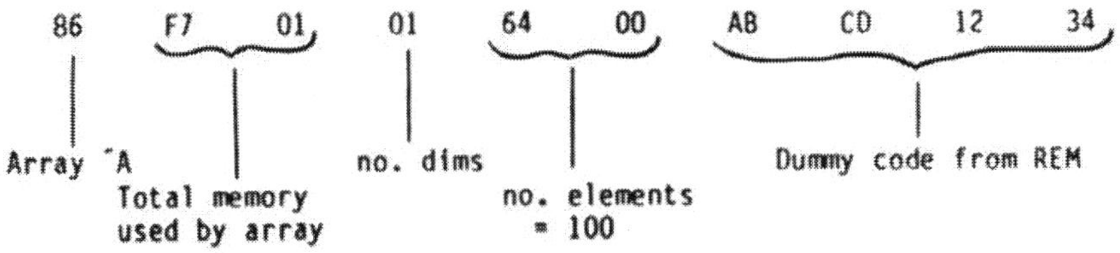

MACHINE CODE:

```
DD 2A 10 40             LD IX, (16400)    START OF ARRAY
01 00 41                LD BC,16640       POINTER BEFORE
                                          LINE 1000
03          FREM        INC BC
0A                      LD A, (BC)
FE EA                   CP EAH            IS THIS REM?
20 FA                   JR NZ,FREM        IF NOT, AGAIN

03          NXTLIN      INC BC
0A                      LD A,(BC)         TAKE 1ST CHAR
D6 1C       NXTCHR      SUB 28            SUBTRACT 28
07                      RCLA
07                      RCLA
07                      RCLA
07                      RCLA              MULTIPLY BY 16
6F                      LD L,A            TEMP STORE
03                      INC B
0A                      LD A,(BC)         NEXT CHAR
D6 1C                   SUB 28            SUBTRACT 28
85                      ADD A,L           ADD VALUE OF
                                          16*1ST CHAR
DD 77 06                LD (IX+6),A       STORE IN ARRAY
DD23                    INC IX
03                      INC BC
0A                      LD A,(BC)         TEST IF END
2E 75                   LD L,75H
2C                      INC L             L=76H
BD                      CP L              END OF LINE?
20 E7                   JR NZ,NXTCHR      IF NOT, GET
                                          NEXT CHAR
03                      INC BC
03                      INC BC
03                      INC BC
03                      INC BC
03                      INC BC            SKIP LINE NO.
0A                      LD A,(BC)
FE EA                   CP EAH            IS IT REM?
C0                      RET NZ            FINISH IF NOT
18 DA                   JR NXTLIN         ELSE GET CHARS
                                          FROM NEXT LINE
```

DRAUGHTS

It is possible for the standard 1K Sinclair ZX81 to play draughts! Of course, this is only possible by using every trick in the book. (A similar machine language program could be written for the ZX80).

The board is shown on the screen as follows:

```
1      1  B     B     B     B
2      B     B     B     B
3      3  B     B     B     B
4
5      5
6      W     W     W     W
7      7  W     W     W     W
8      W     W     W     W

       A  B  C  D  E  F  G  H
```

(The outer numbers 1 - 8 and the designation of columns A - H are not shown on the screen - the only numbering included are the numbers 1,3,5 and 7 as shown within the board).

The rules of the game the ZX81 plays follows the standard rules except that multiple jumps are not allowed and capture is not compulsory.

Reaching the end line results in the creation of a king (shown on the screen as inverse letter), which can only move one square at a time but is allowed to jump backwards.

STRUCTURE OF THE PROGRAM:

In the standard 1K version there is also insufficient room to retain the string variable that initially sets up the board in the program listing. We must therefore resort to putting that string variable in memory and using <GOTO 1> to start the program.

The last space saving "trick" involves replacing all 1- and 2-digit numbers in the listing: each number in a ZX81 listing takes up 6bytes! This is true even if your number is only a single digit. We therefore make liberal use of constructs such as VAL"2" or CODE"W" which only require 4 bytes.

The program is also broken down into 3 different programs, the last two of which overlay the previous ones. This is the only way to enter so much information into the Sinclair ZX81 1K.

The structure is as follows:

Program 1:	PUT MACHINE CODE ROUTINE INTO REM STATEMENT
Program 2:	DEFINE THE BOARD FOR PLAY
Program 3:	DRAW THE BOARD INPUT PLAYER'S MOVE CHECK PLAYER MOVE VALIDITY MAKE COMPUTER'S MOVE (CALL TO USR ROUTINE) GO TO NEXT PLAYER INPUT

DRAUGHTS:

PROGRAM 1:

```
 100 REM 11111111111111111111111
11111111122222222222222222222222
22222222233333333333333333333333
33333333344444444444444444444444
44444444455555555555555555555555
555555555666666666666666
```

The REM statement must have 175 chars in it.

This part of the program is to input the machine language code into the REM statement. The code is listed at the end of this section, commencing at location 4082H = 16514. Use a modified version of the machine code editor to enter this code into the REM statement.

Once you have entered the machine language code, the listing of the machine code editing program is no longer required.

DRAUGHTS

PROGRAM 2

At this stage you should have only line 100 from the program above contianing the machine code.
Add the following lines:

```
120   LET A$ =  "1  B △ B △ B △ B B △ B △ B △ B △
 3  B △ B △ B △  B ▒ △ ▒ △ ▒ △ ▒ △ 5 ▒ △ ▒ △ ▒ △
▒ W △ W △ W  △ W  △ 7 W △ W △ W △W  W △ W △ W △
W     "
```

The graphics character is obtained
by using GRAPHICS and <Shift> <A>

```
150   FOR L = VAL "1" TO VAL "8"
160   PRINT A$ ( TO VAL "8" )
170   LET A$ = A$ ( VAL "9" TO )
180   NEXT L
200   INPUT A$
310   IF USR 16514 > VAL "0" THEN GOTO 200
```

This program will display the board on to the screen and test the machine language routine entered in Program 1.

The screen is saved in the string variable A$, and is printed in 8 lines. It is essential that a minimum configuration screen is set up, so that the structure in memory of the board is as follows:

[&] 1 B B B B [&] B B B B [&] 3 ---

(where the symbol [&] is used to represent END-OF-LINE). If you check this out this means that all legal moves are limited to increases and decreases of 8 or 10 bytes in memory.

Users with additional memory connected to the ZX81 should add the following lines:

```
     130  POKE 16389, 76
     140  CLS
```

This will ensure that a minimum configuration screen is set up.

RUNNING PROGRAM 2

Press <RUN>. The screen will be displayed as shown above, and the ZX81 will be waiting for a string input. Press <NEW LINE> to see the computer's first move. You should see the computer move its first piece from G3 to H4.

You can continue to press <NEW LINE> to see what the computer would do next if that was its position. If you so desire you can change the string variable in 120 to set up any starting position.

PREPARING FOR PROGRAM 3

Enter the following line into your listing:

```
130 STOP
```

and then press <RUN>. Delete lines 120 and 130 and SAVE your program so far.

This has the effect of storing the string variable in memory without the need to keep it in the program listing. (Users with more than 1K memory do not need to do this - retain your original lines 120 - 140).

DRAUGHTS
PROGRAM 3

At this stage you should have lines 100, lines 150 - 180, and lines 200 and 310. The string variable A$ is stored in memory, so do not press <RUN> or <CLEAR> as this will destroy the contents of A$.

Add the following lines to your program:

```
210  LET S = PEEK 16396 + VAL "256" * PEEK 16397
220  LET F = S + CODE A$ + VAL "9" * CODE A$
     (VAL "2" ) - VAL "298"
230  LET T = S + CODE A$ ( VAL "3" ) + VAL "9" *
     CODE A$ ( VAL "4" ) - VAL "298"
240  LET M = (T + F) / VAL "2"
250  IF (PEEK F <> CODE "W" AND PEEK F <> CODE
     "W") OR (ABS (F-T) > VAL "10" AND PEEK M <>
```

```
    CODE "B" AND PEEK M <> CODE "█" > OR (PEEK F
    < CODE "X" AND F<T ) OR PEEK T <> CODE "█" THEN
    GOTO 200
                      Letters in squares are inverse
                      characters obtained using GRAPHICS
                      mode.
270 POKE T, CODE "W" + CODE "█" * (PEEK F )
    CODE "W" OR (T-S) < VAL "9")
                      The graphic character in this line
                      is obtained in GRAPHICS mode by
                      pressing <Space>
280 POKE F, CODE "█"
290 IF ABS (F-T) > VAL  "10" THEN POKE M, CODE "█"
300 PAUSE CODE "W"
```

PLAYING DRAUGHTS:

As we mentioned at the beginning, if you only have 1K you cannot use <RUN> as this will clear the variable so carefully saved. Use <GOTO 1> instead. (Users with additional memory have the string variable in the listing so can use <RUN>.)

You should already have tested Program 2 by the time you come to this point, so you already know the display routine works and the machine language routine works. The additions in Program 3 are the player's moves and checking if these moves are allowed (This is all in line 250: "F" is "from" and "T" is "to").

The input the computer is waiting for is a 4-character string, such as "A6B5". This means that you mean to move from square A6 to square B5.

As only the most rudimentary numbering has been included in the screen, you may find it useful to keep a properly numbered board by the computer when playing.

If you should wish to play a second game, you cannot simply use <GOTO 1> again, as the string variable A$ has been deleted from memory. You will need to either reload the program from cassette or re-enter on the edit line the string variable A$ as in line 120. You can use this to also enter different positions you wish to examine - eg. giving the computer a head start.

```
                00100 ;
                00110 ;           Z81 DRAUGHTS PROGRAM
                00120 ;
4082            00130             ORG     16514
                00140 ;
403C            00150 FROM        EQU     16444
403E            00160 TO          EQU     16446
4040            00170 CAPFRM      EQU     16448
4042            00180 CAPTO       EQU     16450
4044            00190 CAPT        EQU     16452
                00200 ;
                00210 ;
0008            00220 BLANK       EQU     8           ;CODE FOR EMPTY
0027            00230 BLACK       EQU     39          ;CODE FOR 'B'
003C            00240 WHITE       EQU     60          ;CODE FOR 'W'
                00250 ;
                00260 ;
                00270 ;
                00280 ;           MAIN PROGRAM
                00290 ;
4082 AF         00300 START       XOR     A
4083 213C40     00310             LD      HL,FROM             ;CANCEL O
4086 060A       00320             LD      B,10                ;MOVES FR
4088 77         00330 CLEAR       LD      (HL),A              ;MEMORY
4089 23         00340             INC     HL
408A 10FC       00350             DJNZ    CLEAR
                00360 ;
408C 0648       00370             LD      B,72                ;B=BOARD
408E 2A0C40     00380             LD      HL,(16396)          ;HL =) BO
4091 E5         00390             PUSH    HL                  ;   SAVE
                00400 ;
                00410 ;
                00420 ;           THIS SECTION CHECKS EACH PIECE
                00430 ;           ON THE BOARD FOR POSSIBLE MOVES
                00440 ;
                00450 ;           IF POSITION HAS BLACK PIECE OR
                00460 ;           BLACK KING, SUBROUTINE TEST IS
                00470 ;           CALLED TO SEE IF ANY POSSIBLE
                00480 ;           MOVES OR CAPTURES EXIST.
                00490 ;
4092 7E         00500 NEXT        LD      A,(HL)
4093 FEA7       00510             CP      BLACK+128   ;IS IT OUR KIN
4095 2812       00520             JR      Z,KNGFND    ; YES =) KING F
4097 FE27       00530             CP      BLACK       ;IS IT PIECE ?
4099 201A       00540             JR      NZ,ENDSCH   ; NO =) TRY NEX
409B 110800     00550 MANFND      LD      DE,8        ;
409E CDF140     00560             CALL    TEST        ;   JUMPS FOR
40A1 110A00     00570             LD      DE,10
40A4 CDF140     00580             CALL    TEST        ;       BLACK PIEC
40A7 180C       00590             JR      ENDSCH
40A9 11F6FF     00600 KNGFND      LD      DE,-10
40AC CDF140     00610             CALL    TEST        ;   JUMPS FOR
40AF 11F8FF     00620             LD      DE,-8
40B2 CDF140     00630             CALL    TEST        ;       BLACK KING
40B5 23         00640 ENDSCH      INC     HL          ;MOVE TO NEXT POS
40B6 10DA       00650             DJNZ    NEXT        ;CONTINUE IF NOT
                00660 ;
                00670 ;
40B8 113C40     00680 MOVEIT      LD      DE,FROM ;ROUTINE TO SHIFT
40BB 214340     00690             LD      HL,CAPTO+1  ;CAPFRM & CAP
```

```
34                    INC    (HL)          ;TO "FROM" & "TO"
35                    DEC    (HL)          ;IF CAPTURE POSS
010400                LD     BC,4
2002                  JR     NZ,CAPOK
0E00                  LD     C,0
D5          CAPOK     PUSH   DE
D5                    PUSH   DE
E1                    POP    HL
09                    ADD    HL,BC
0E04                  LD     C,4
EDB0                  LDIR
            ;
            ;
CD2C41                CALL   FILL      ;FILL IN CAPTURE
3608                  LD     (HL),BLANK
E1                    POP    HL
CD2C41                CALL   FILL      ;FILL IN "FROM"
7E                    LD     A,(HL)
3608                  LD     (HL),BLANK
13                    INC    DE
EB                    EX     DE,HL
CD2C41                CALL   FILL      ;FIND POS "TO"
D1                    POP    DE
013F00                LD     BC,63     ;CHECK IF KING
EB                    EX     DE,HL     ;HAS BEEN
09                    ADD    HL,BC     ;CREATED BY MOVE
EB                    EX     DE,HL
E5                    PUSH   HL
ED52                  SBC    HL,DE
E1                    POP    HL
3802                  JR     C,NOKING   ; C => NO KING
F680                  OR     80H
77          NOKING    LD     (HL),A
            ;
C9                    RET          ;END OF MAIN ROUTINE
            ;
            ;
            ;
            ;         TEST SUBROUTINE
            ;
            ;
            ;         THIS SUBROUTINE RETURNS ALL
            ;         REGISTERS UNCHANGED EXCEPT
            ;         FOR REGISTER 'A'
            ;
            ;         IF LEGAL POSSIBLE IT IS RECORDED
            ;         IF CAPTURE POSSIBLE, RECORDED
            ;
            ;         LEGAL MOVES WHICH WOULD LEAD TO
            ;         IMMEDIATE CAPTURE ARE ONLY
            ;         RECORDED IF NO OTHER LEGAL
            ;         MOVE HAS BEEN FOUND TO DATE
            ;
            ;
            ;
E5          TEST      PUSH   HL        ;SAVE COMPUTER POS
19                    ADD    HL,DE
7E                    LD     A,(HL)
FE08                  CP     BLANK     ;IS MOVE TO EMPTY?
2012                  JR     NZ,ENEMY   ;IF NOT IS CAPT OK?
```

```
40F8 E5        01300              PUSH    HL
40F9 19        01310              ADD     HL,DE    ;WALKING INTO TRA
40FA 7E        01320              LD      A,(HL)
40FB E67F      01330              AND     7FH
40FD FE3C      01340              CP      WHITE    ;ENEMY MAN OR KIN
40FF 2822      01350              JR      Z,LAST   ;IF TRAP MOVE ONL
               01360                               ;AS LAST RESORT
4101 E1        01370 MOVE         POP     HL
4102 223E40    01380              LD      (TO),HL
4105 E1        01390              POP     HL
4106 223C40    01400              LD      (FROM),HL
4109 C9        01410              RET     ;POSSIBLE MOVE RECORDED
               01420 ;
410A E67F      01430 ENEMY        AND     7FH
410C FE3C      01440              CP      WHITE    ;CAN WE CAPTURE?
410E 201A      01450              JR      NZ,LOSE1 ;IF NOT, FORGET
4110 E5        01460              PUSH    HL
4111 19        01470              ADD     HL,DE
4112 7E        01480              LD      A,(HL)
4113 FE08      01490              CP      BLANK    ;IS CAPTURE POSS?
4115 2012      01500              JR      NZ,LOSE2 ;NEVER MIND
4117 224240    01510              LD      (CAPTO),HL
411A E1        01520              POP     HL
411B 224440    01530              LD      (CAPT),HL
411E E1        01540              POP     HL
411F 224040    01550              LD      (CAPFRM),HL
4122 C9        01560              RET              ;CAPTURE RECORDED
               01570 ;
4123 3A3F40    01580 LAST         LD      A,(TO+1)
4126 A7        01590              AND     A
4127 28D8      01600              JR      Z,MOVE   ;NO OTHER MOVES E
4129 E1        01610 LOSE2        POP     HL       ;DON'T RECORD
412A E1        01620 LOSE1        POP     HL
412B C9        01630              RET
               01640 ;
               01650 ;
               01660 ;
               01670 ;            SUBROUTINE TO FIND POSITION
               01680 ;            TO BE FILLED NEXT
               01690 ;
               01700 ;            THIS SUBROUTINE LOADS HL WITH (HL
               01710 ;            INPUT: HL VARIABLE WHERE POS IS S
               01720 ;            OUTPUT: HL CONTAINS POS STORED
               01730 ;            DESTROYED: DE IS CHANGED BY SUBRO
               01740 ;               (ON RETURN CONTAINS VARIABLE+1
               01750 ;
412C 5E        01760 FILL         LD      E,(HL)
412D 23        01770              INC     HL
412E 56        01780              LD      D,(HL)
412F EB        01790              EX      DE,HL
4130 C9        01800              RET
               01810 ;
               01820 ;
0000           01830              END
00000 TOTAL ERRORS
```

FLAG OPERATION SUMMARY TABLE

INSTRUCTION	C	Z	P/V	S	N	H	COMMENTS
ADC HL, SS	#	#	V	#	Ø	X	16-bit add with carry
ADX s; ADD s	#	#	V	#	Ø	#	8-bit add or add with carry
ADD DD, SS	#	—	—	—	Ø	X	16-bit add
AND s	Ø	#	P	#	Ø	1	Logical operations
BIT b, s	—	#	X	X	Ø	1	State of bit b of location s is copied into the Z flag
CCF	#	—	—	—	Ø	X	Complement carry
CPD; CPDR; CPI; CPIR	—	#	#	X	1	X	Block search instruction Z=1 if A=(HL), else Z=Ø P/V=1 if BC≠Ø, otherwise P/V=Ø
CP s	#	#	V	#	1	#	Compare accumulator
CPL	—	—	—	—	1	1	Complement accumulator
DAA	#	#	P	#	—	#	Decimal adjust accumulator
DEC s	—	#	V	#	1	#	8-bit decrement
IN r, (C)	—	#	P	#	Ø	Ø	Input register indirect
INC s	—	#	V	#	Ø	#	8-bit increment
IND; INI	—	#	X	X	1	X	Block input Z=Ø if B≠Ø else Z=1
INDR:INIR	—	1	X	X	1	X	Block input Z=Ø if B≠Ø else Z=1
LD A,I ; LD A,R	—	#	IFF	#	Ø	Ø	Content of interrupt enable Flip-Flop is copied into the P/V flag
LDD; LDI	—	X	#	X	Ø	Ø	Block transfer instructions
LDDR; LDIR	—	X	Ø	X	Ø	Ø	P/V=1 if BC≠Ø, otherwise P/V=Ø
NEG	#	#	V	#	1	#	Negate accumulator
OR s	Ø	#	P	#	Ø	Ø	Logical OR accumulator
OTDR; OTIR	—	1	X	X	1	X	Block output; Z=Ø if B≠Ø otherwise Z=1
OUTD; OUTI	—	#	X	X	1	X	Block output; Z=Ø if B≠Ø otherwise Z=1
RLA; RLCA; RRA; RRCA	#	—	—	—	Ø	Ø	Rotate accumulator
RLD; RRD	—	#	P	#	Ø	/	Rotate digit left and right
RLS; RLC s; RR s; RRC s SLA s; SRA s; SRL s	#	#	P	#	Ø	Ø	Rotate and shift location s
SBC HL, SS	#	#	V	#	1	X	16-bit subtract with carry
SCF	1	—	—	—	Ø	Ø	Set carry
SBC s; SUB s			V		1		8-bit subtract with carry
XOR x	Ø		P		Ø	Ø	Exclusive OR accumulator

SYMBOL	OPERATION
C	Carry flag. C=1 if the operation produced a carry from the most significant bit of the operand or result.
Z	Zero flag. Z=1 if the result of the operation is zero.
S	Sign flag. S=1 if the most significant bit of the result is one, ie a negative number.
P/V	Parity or overflow flag. Parity (P) and overflow (O) share the same flag. Logical operations affect this flag with the parity of the result while arithmetic operations affect this flag with the overflow of the result. If P/V holds parity, P/V=1 if the result of the operation is even, P/V=0 if result is odd. If P/V holds overflow, P/V=1 if the result of the operation produced an overflow.
H	Half-carry flag. H=1 if the add or subtract operation produced a carry into or borrow from bit 4 of the accumulator.
N	Add/Subtract flag. N=1 if the previous operations was a subtract. H and N flags are used in conjunction with the decimal adjust instruction (DAA) to properly correct the result into packed BCD format following addition or subtractionusing operands with packed BCD format.
#	The flag is affected according to the result of the operation.
-	The flag is unchanged by the operation.
0	The flag is reset (=0) by the operation.
1	The flag is set (=1) by the operation.
X	The flag result is unknown.
V	The P/V flag is affected according to the overflow result of the operation.
P	P/V flag is affected according to the parity result of the operation.
r	Any one of the CPU registers A,B,C,D,E,H,L.
s	Any 8-bit location for all the addressing modes allowed for the particular instructions.
SS	Any 16-bit location for all the addressing modes allowed for that instruction.
R	Refresh register
n	8-bit value in range 0-255.
nn	16-bit value in range 0-65535.

Z80–CPU INSTRUCTIONS SORTED BY OP-CODE

HEXADECIMAL	MNEMONIC	HEXADECIMAL	MNEMONIC	HEXADECIMAL	MNEMONIC
00	NOP	49	LD C,C	92	SUB D
01 XXXX	LD BC,NN	4A	LD C,D	93	SUB E
02	LD (BC),A	4B	LD C,E	94	SUB H
03	INC BC	4C	LD C,H	95	SUB L
04	INC B	4D	LD C,L	96	SUB (HL)
05	DEC B	4E	LD C,(HL)	97	SUB A
06XX	LD B,N	4F	LD C,A	98	SBC A,B
07	RLCA	50	LD D,B	99	SBC A,C
08	EX AF, AF'	51	LD D,C	9A	SBC A,D
09	ADD HL,BC	52	LD D,D	9B	SBC A,E
0A	LD A, (BC)	53	LD D,E	9C	SBC A,H
0B	DEC BC	54	LD D,H	9D	SBC A,L
0C	INC C	55	LD D,L	9E	SBC A,(HL)
0D	DEC C	56	LD D,(HL)	9F	SBC A,A
0EXX	LD C,N	57	LD D,A	A0	AND B
0F	RRCA	58	LD E,B	A1	AND C
10XX	DJNZ DIS	59	LD E,C	A2	AND C
11XXXX	LD DE,NN	5A	LD E,D	A3	AND E
12	LD (DE),A	5B	LD E,E	A4	AND H
13	INC DE	5C	LD E,H	A5	AND L
14	INC D	5D	LD E,L	A6	AND (HL)
15	DEC D	5E	LD E,(HL)	A7	AND A
16XX	LD D,N	5F	LD E,A	A8	XOR B
17	RLA	60	LD H,B	A9	XOR C
18XX	JR DIS	61	LD H,C	AA	SOR D
19	ADD HL,DE	62	LD H,D	AB	XOR E
1A	LD A,(DE)	63	LD H,E	AC	SOR H
1B	DEC DE	64	LD H,H	AD	SOR L
1C	INC E	65	LD H,L	AE	XOR (HL)
1D	DEC E	66	LD H,(HL)	AF	XOR A
1EXX	LD E,N	67	LD H,A	B0	OR B
1F	RRA	68	LD L,B	B1	OR C
20XX	JR NZ,DIS	69	LD L,C	B2	OR D
21XXXX	LD HL,NN	6A	LD L,D	B3	OR E
22XXXX	LD (NN),HL	6B	LD L,E	B4	OR H
23	INC HL	6C	LD L,H	B5	OR L
24	INC H	6D	LD L,L	B6	OR (HL)
25	DEC H	6E	LD L,(HL)	B7	OR A
26XX	LD H,N	6F	LD L,A	B8	CP B
27	DAA	70	LD (HL),B	B9	CP C
28XX	JR Z,DIS	71	LD (HL),C	BA	CP D
29	ADD HL,HL	72	LD (HL),D	BB	CP E
2AXXXX	LD HL,(NN)	73	LD (HL),E	BC	CP H
2B	DEC HL	74	LD (HL),H	BD	CP L
2C	INC L	75	LD (HL),L	BE	CP (HL)
2D	DEC L	76	HALT	BF	CP A
2EXX	LD L,N	77	LD (HL),A	C0	RET NZ
2F	CPL	78	LD A,B	C1	POP BC
30XX	JR NC,DIS	79	LD A,C	C2XXXX	JP NZ,NM
31XXXX	LD SP,NN	7A	LD A,D	C3XXXX	JP NM
32XXXX	LD (NN),A	7B	LD A,E	C4XXXX	CALL NZ,NM
33	INC SP	7C	LD A,H	C5	PUSH BC
34	INC (HL)	7D	LD A,L	C6XX	ADD A,N
35	DEC (HL)	7E	LD A,(HL)	C7	RST 0
3620XX	LD (HL),N	7F	LD A,A	C8	RET Z
37	SCF	80	ADD A,B	C9	RET
38XX	JR C,DIS	81	ADD A,C	CAXXXX	JP Z,NM
39	ADD HL,SP	82	ADD A,D	CCXXXX	CALL Z,NN
3AXXXX	LD A,(NN)	83	ADD A,E	CDXXXX	CALL NN
3B	DEC SP	84	ADD A,H	CEXX	ADC A,N
3C	INC A	85	ADD A,L	CF	RST 8
3D	DEC A	86	ADD A,(HL)	D0	RET NC
3EXXXX	LD A	87	ADD A,A	D1	POP DE
3F	CCF	88	ADC A,B	D2XXXX	JP NC,NN
40	LD B,B	89	ADC A,C	D3XX	OUT (N),A
41	LD B,C	8A	ADC A,D	D4XXXX	CALL NC,NN
42	LD B,D	8B	ADC A,E	D5	PUSH DE
43	LD B,E	8C	ADC A,H	D6XX	SUB N
44	LD B,H,	8D	ADC A,L	D7	RST 10H
45	LD B,L	8E	ADC A,(HL)	D8	RET C
46	LD B,(HL)	8F	ADC A,A	D9	EXX
47	LD B,A	90	SUB B	DAXXXX	JP C,NN
48	LD C,B	91	SUB C	DBXX	IN A,(N)

HEXADECIMAL	MNEMONIC	HEXADECIMAL	MNEMONIC	HEXADECIMAL	MNEMONIC
DCXXXX	CALL C,NN	CB28	SRA B	CB79	BIT 7,C
DEXX	SBC A,N	CB29	SRA C	CB7A	BIT 7,D
DF	RST 18H	CB2A	SRA D	CB7B	BIT 7,E
E0	RET PO	CB2B	SRA E	CB7C	BIT 7,H
E1	POP HL	CB2C	SRA H	CB7D	BIT 7,L
E2XXXX	JP PO,NN	CB2D	SRA L	CB7E	BIT 7,(HL)
E3	EX (SP),HL	CB2E	SRA (HL)	CB7F	BIT 7,A
E4XXXX	CALL PO,NN	CB2F	SRA A	CB80	RES 0,B
E5	PUSH HL	CB38	SRL B	CB81	RES 0,C
E6XX	AND N	CB39	SRL C	CB82	RES 0,D
E7	RST 20 H	CB3A	SRL D	CB83	RES 0,E
E8	RET PE	CB3B	SRL E	CB84	RES 0,H
E9	JP (HL)	CB3C	SRL H	CB85	RES 0,L
EAXXXX	JE PE NN	CB3D	SRL L	CB86	RES 0,(HL)
EB	EX DE,HL	CB3E	SRL (HL)	CB87	RES 0,A
ECXXXX	CALL PE,NN	CB3F	SRL A	CB88	RES 1,B
EEXX	XOR N	CB40	BIT 0,B	CB89	RES 1,C
EF	RST 28H	CB41	BIT 0,C	CB8A	RES 1,D
F0	RET P	CB42	BIT 0,D	CB8B	RES 1,E
F1	POP AF	CB43	BIT 0,E	CB8C	RES 1,H
F2XXXX	JR P,NN	CB44	bit 0,H	CB8D	RES 1,L
F3	D1	CB45	BIT 0,L	CB8E	RES 1,(HL)
F4XXXX	CALL P,NN	CB46	BIT 0,(HL)	CB8F	RES 1,A
F5	PUSH AF	CB47	BIT 0,A	CB90	RES 2,B
F620XX	OR N	CB48	Bit 1,B	CB91	RES 2,C
F7	RST 30H	CB49	BIT 1,C	CB92	RES 2,D
F8	RET N	CB4A	BIT 1,D	CB93	RES 2,E
F9	LD,SP,HL	CB4B	BIT 1,E	CB94	RES 2,H
FAXXXX	JP N,NN	CB4C	BIT 1,H	CB95	RES 2,L
FB	E1	CB4D	BIT 1,L	CB96	RES 2,(HL)
FCXXXX	CALL M,NN	CB4E	BIT 1,(HL)	CB97	RES 2,A
FE20XX	CP N	CB4F	BIT 1,A	CB98	RES 3,B
FF	RST 38H	CB50	BIT 2,B	CB99	RES 3,C
CB00	RLC 8	CB51	BIT 2,C	CB9A	RES 3,D
CB01	RLC C	CB52	BIT 2,D	CB9B	RES 3,E
CB02	RLC D	CB53	BIT 2,E	CB9C	RES e,H
CB03	RLC E	CB54	BIT 2,H	CB9D	RES 3,L
CB04	RLC H	CB55	BIT 2,L	CB9E	RES 3,(HL)
CB05	RLC L	CB56	BIT 2,(HL)	CB9F	RES 3,A
CB06	RLC (HL)	CB57	BIT 2,A	CBA0	RES 4,B
CB07	RLC A	CB58	BIT 3,B	CBA1	RES 4,C
CB08	RRC B	CB59	BIT 3,C	CBA2	RES 4,D
CB09	RRC C	CB5A	BIT 3,D	CBA3	RES e,E
CB0A	RRC D	CB5B	BIT 3,E	CBA4	RES e,H
CB0B	RRC E	CB5C	BIT 3,H	CBA5	RES 4,L
CB0C	RRC H	CB5D	BIT 3,L	CBA6	RES 4,(HL)
CB0D	RRC L	CB5E	BIT 3,(HL)	CBA7	RES 4,A
CB0E	RRC (HL)	CB5F	BIT 3,A	CBA8	RES 5,B
CB0F	RRC A	CB60	BIT 4,B	CBA9	RES 5,C
CB10	RL B	CB61	BIT 4,C	CBAA	RES 5,D
CB11	RL C	CB62	BIT 4,D	CBAB	RES 5,E
CB12	RL D	CB63	BIT 4,E	CBAC	RES 5,H
CB13	RL E	CB64	BIT 4,H	CBAD	RES 5,L
CB14	RL H	CB65	BIT 4,L	CBAE	RES 5,(HL)
CB15	RL L	CB66	BIT 4,(HL)	CBAF	RES 5,A
CB16	RL (HL)	CB67	BIT 4,A	CBB0	RES 6,B
CB17	RL A	CB68	BIT 5,B	CBB1	RES 6,C
CB18	RR B	CB69	BIT 5,C	CBB2	RES 6,D
CB19	RR C	CB6A	BIT 5,D	CBB3	RES 6,E
CB1A	RR D	CB6B	BIT 5,E	CBB4	RES 6,H
CB1B	RR E	CB6C	BIT 5,H	CBB5	RES 6,L
CB1C	RR H	CB6D	BIT 5,L	CBB6	RES 6,(HL)
CB1D	RR L	CB6E	BIT 5,(HL)	CBB7	RES 7,A
CB1E	RR (HL)	CB6F	BIT 5,A	CBB8	RES 7,B
CB1F	RR A	CB70	BIT 6,B	CBB9	RES 7,C
CB20	SLA B	CB71	BIT 6,C	CBBA	RES 7,D
CB21	SLA C	CB72	BIT 6,D	CBBB	RES 7,E
CB22	SKA D	CB73	BIT 6,E	CBBC	RES 7,H
CB23	SLA E	CB74	BIT 6,H	CBBD	RES 7,L
CB24	SLA H	CB75	BIT 6,L	CBBE	RES 7,(HL)
CB25	SLA L	CB76	BIT 6,(HL)	CBBF	RES 7,A
CB26	SLA (HL)	CB77	BIT 6,A	CBC0	SET 0,B
CB27	SLA A	CB78	BIT 7,B	CBC1	SET 0,C
				CBC2	SET 0,D

HEXADECIMAL	MNEMONIC	HEXADECIMAL	MNEMONIC	HEXADECIMAL	MNEMONIC
CBC3	SET 0,E	DD4EXX	LD C,(IX+d)	ED56	IN 1
CBC4	SET 0,H	DD56XX	LD D,(IX+d)	ED57	LD A,1
CBC5	SET 0,L	DD5EXX	LD E,(IX+d)	ED58	IN E,(C)
CBC6	SET 0,(HL)	DD66XX	LD H,(IX+d)	ED59	OUT (C),E
CBC7	SET 0,A	DD6EXX	LD L,(IX+d)	ED5A	ADC HL,DE
CBC8	SET 1,B	DD70XX	LD (IX+d),B	ED5BXXXX	LD DE,(NN)
CBC9	SET 1,C	DD71XX	LD (IC+d),C	ED5E	IM 2
CBCA	SET 1,D	DD72XX	LD (IX+d),D	ED60	IN H,(C)
CBCB	SET 1,E	DD73XX	LD (IX+d),E	ED61	OUT(C),H
CBCC	SET 1,H	DD74XX	LD (IX+d),H	ED62	SBC HL,HL
CBCD	SET 1,L	DD75XX	LD (IX+d),L	ED67	RRD
CBCE	SET 1,(HL)	DD77XX	LD (IX+d),A	ED68	IN L,(C)
CBCF	SET 1,A	DD7EXX	LD A,(IX+d)	ED69	OUT(C),L
CBD0	SET 2,B	DD86XX	ADD A,(IX+d)	ED6A	ADC HL,HL
CBD1	SET 2,C	DD8EXX	ADC A,(IX+d)	ED6F	RLD
CBD2	SET 2,D	DD96XX	SUB(IX+d)	ED72	SBC HL,SP
CBD3	SET 2,E	DD9EXX	SBC A,(IX+d)	ED73XXXX	LD(NN),SP
CBD4	SET 2,H	DDA6XX	AND(IX+d)	ED78	IN A,(C)
CBD5	SET 2,L	DDAEXX	XOR(IX+d)	ED79	OUT(C),A
CBD6	SET 2,(HL)	DDB6XX	OR(IX+d)	ED7A	ADC HL,SP
CBD7	SET 2,A	DDBEXX	CP(IX+d)	ED7BXXXX	LD SP,(NN)
CBD8	SET 3,B	DDE1	POP IX	EDA0	LDI
CBD9	SET 3,C	DDE3	EX(SP),IX	EDA1	CPI
CBDA	SET 3,D	DDE5	PUSH IX	EDA2	INI
CBDB	SET 3,E	DDE9	JP(IX)	EDA3	OUTI
CBDC	SET 3,H	DDF9	LD SP,IX	EDA8	LDD
CBDD	SET 3,L	DDCBXX06	RLC(IX+d)	EDA9	CPD
CBDE	SET 3,(HL)	DDCBXX0E	RRC(IX+d)	EDAA	IND
CBDF	SET 3,A	DDCBXX16	RL(IX+d)	EDAB	OUTD
CBE0	SET 4,B	DDCBXX1E	RR(IX+d)	ED80	LDIR
CBE1	SET 4,C	DDCBXX26	SLA(IX+d)	ED81	CPIR
CBE2	SET 4,D	DDCBXX2E	SRA(IX+d)	ED82	INIR
CBE3	SET 4,E	DDCBXX3E	SRL(IX+d)	ED83	OTIR
CBE4	SET 4,H	DDCBXX46	BIT 0,(IX+d)	ED88	LDDR
CBE5	SET 4,L	DDCBXX4E	BIT 1,(IX+d)	ED89	CPDR
CBE6	SET 4,(HL)	DDCBXX56	BIT 2,(IX+d)	ED8A	INDR
CBE7	SET 4,A	DDCBXX5E	BIT 3,(IX+d)	ED8B	OTDR
CBE8	SET 5,B	DDCBXX66	BIT 4,(IX+d)	ED09	ADD IV,BC
CBE9	SET 5,C	DDCBXX6E	BIT 5,(IX+d)	ED19	ADD IV,DC
CBEA	SET 5,D	DDCBXX76	BIT 6,(IX+d)	ED21XXXX	LD IV,NN
CBEB	SET 5,E	DDCBXX7E	BIT 7,(IX+d)	FD22XXXX	LD(NN),IV
CBEC	SET 5,H	DDCBXX86	RES 0,(IX+d)	FD23	INC IY
CBED	SET 5,L	DDCBXX8E	RES 1,(IX+d)	FD29	ADD IY,IY
CBEE	SET 5,(HL)	DDCBXX96	RES 2,(IX+d)	FD2AXXXX	LD IY,(NN)
CBEF	SET 5,A	DDCBXX9E	RES 3,(IX+d)	FD2B	DEC IY
CBF0	SET 6,B	DDCBXXA6	RES 4,(IX+d)	FD34XX	INC(IY+d)
CBF1	SET 6,C	DDCBXXAE	RES 5,(IX+d)	FD35XX	DEC(IY+d)
CBF2	SET 6,D	DDCBXXB6	RES 6,(IX+d)	FD36XX20	LD(IY+d),N
CBF3	SET 6,E	DDCBXXBE	RES 7,(IX+d)	FD39	ADD IY,SP
CBF4	SET 6,H	DDCBXXC6	SET 0,(IX+d)	FD46XX	LD B,(IY+d)
CBF5	SET 6,L	DDCBXXCE	SET 1,(IX+d)	FD3EXX	LD C,(IY+d)
CBF6	SET 6,(HL)	DDCBXXD6	SET 2,(IX+d)	FD56XX	LD D,(IY+d)
CBF7	SET 6,A	DDCBXXDE	SET 3,(IX+d)	FD5EXX	LD E,(IY+d)
CBF8	SET 7,B	DDCBXXE6	SET 4,(IX+d)	FD66XX	LD H,(IY+d)
CBF9	SET 7,C	DDCBXXEE	SET 5,(IX+d)	FD6EXX	LD L,(IY+d)
CBFA	SET 7,D	DDCBXXF6	SET 6,(IX+d)	FD70XX	LD (IY+d),B
CBFB	SET 7,E	DDCBXXFE	SET 7,(IX+d)	FD71XX	LD (IY+d),C
CBFC	SET 7,H	ED40	IN B,(C)	FD72XX	LD (IY+d),D
CBFD	SET 7,L	ED41	OUT(C),B	FD73XX	LD (IY+d),E
CBFE	SET 7,(HL)	ED42	SBC HL,BC	FD74XX	LD (IY+d),H
CBFF	SET 7,A	ED43XXXX	LD(NN),BC	FD75XX	LD (IY+d),L
DD09	ADD IX,BC	ED44	NEG	FD77XX	LD (IY+d),A
DD19	ADD IX,DE	ED45	RETN	FD7EXX	LD A,(IY+d)
DD21XXXX	LD IX,NN	ED46	IM 0	FD86XX	ADD A,(IY+d)
DD22XXXX	LD(NN),IX	ED47	LD 1,A	FD8EXX	ADC A,(IY+d)
DD23	INC IX	ED48	IN C,(C)	FD96XX	SUB(IY+d)
DD29	ADD IX,IX	ED49	OUT(C) ,C	FD9EXX	SBC A,(IY+d)
DD2AXXXX	LD IX,(NN)	ED4A	ADC HL,BC	FDA6XX	AND (IY+d)
DD2B	DEC IX	ED4BXXXX	LD BC,(NN)	FDAEXX	XOR (IY+d)
DD34XX	INC(IX+d)	ED4D	RET1	FDB6XX	OR (IY+d)
DD35XX	DEC(IX+d)	ED50	IN D,(C)	FDBEXX	CP (IY+d)
DD36XX20	LD(IX+d),N	ED51	OUT(C),D	FDE1	POP IY
DD39	ADD IX,SP	ED52	SBC HL,DE	FDE3	EX (SP), IY
DD46XX	LD B,(IX+d)	ED53XXXX	LD(NN),DE		

HEXADECIMAL	MNEMONIC	HEXADECIMAL	MNEMONIC	HEXADECIMAL	MNEMONIC
FDE5	PUSH IY				
FDE9	JP (IY)				
FDF9	LD SP,IY				
FDCBXX06	RLC(IY+d)				
FDCBXX0E	RRC(IY+d)				
FDCBXX16	RL(IY+d)				
FDCBXX1E	RR(IY+d)				
FDCBXX26	SLA(IY+d)				
FDCBXX2E	SRA(IY+d)				
FDCBXX3E	SRL(IY+d)				
FDCBXX46	BIT 0,(IY+d)				
FDCBXX4E	BIT 1,(IY+d)				
FDCBXX56	BIT 2,(IY+d)				
FDCBXX5E	BIT 3,(IY+d)				
FDCBXX66	BIT 4,(IY+d)				
FDCBXX6E	BIT 5,(IT+d)				
FDCBXX76	BIT 6,(IY+d)				
FDCBXX7E	BIT 7,(IY+d)				
FDCBXX86	RES 0,(IY+d)				
FDCBXX8E	RES 1,(IY+d)				
FDCBXX96	RES 2,(IY+d)				
FDCBXX9E	RES 3,(IY+d)				
FDCBXXA6	RES 4,(IY+d)				
FDCBXXAE	RES 5,(IY+d)				
FDCBXXB6	RES 6,(IY+d)				
FDCBXXBE	RES 7,(IY+d)				
FDCBXXC6	SET 0,(IY+d)				
FDCBXXCE	SET 1,(IY+d)				
FDCBXXD6	SET 2,(IY+d)				
FDCBXXDE	SET 3,(IY+d)				
FDCBXXE6	SET 4,(IY+d)				
FDCBXXEE	SET 5,(IY+d)				
FDCBXXF6	SET 6,(IY+d)				
FDCBXXFE	SET 7,(IY+d)				

Z80–CPU INSTRUCTIONS SORTED BY MNEMONIC

MNEMONIC	HEXADECIMAL
ADC A, (HL)	8E
ADC A, (IX+dis)	DD 8E XX
ADC A,(IY+dis)	FD 8E xx
ADC A,A	8F
ADC A,B	88
ADC A,C	89
ADC A,D	8A
ADC A,n	CE XX
ADC A,E	8B
ADC A,H	8C
ADC A,L	8D
ADC HL,BC	ED 4A
ADC HL,DE	ED 5A
ADC HL,HL	ED 6A
ADC HL,SP	ED 7A
ADD A, (HL)	86
ADD A,(IX+dis)	DD 86XX
ADD A,(IY+dis)	FD 86XX
ADD A,A	87
ADD A,B	80
ADD A,C	81
ADD A,D	82
ADD A,n	C6 XX
ADD A,E	83
ADD A,H	84
ADD A,L	85
ADD HL,BC	09
ADD HL,DE	19
ADD HL,HL	29
ADD HL,SP	39
ADD IX,BC	DD 09
ADD IX,DE	DD 19
ADD IX,IX	DD 29
ADD IX,SP	DD 39
ADD IY,BC	FD 09
ADD IY,DE	FD 19
ADD IY,IY	FD 29
ADD IY,SP	FD 39
AND (HL)	A6
AND (IX+dis)	DD A6 XX
AND (IY+dis)	FD A6 XX
AND A	A7
AND B	A0
AND C	A1
AND D	A2
AND n	E6 XX
AND E	A3
AND H	A4
AND L	A5
BIT 0;(HL)	CB 46
BIT 0,(IX+dis)	DD CB XX 46
BIT 0,(IY+dis)	FD CB XX 46
BIT 0,A	CB 47
BIT o,B	CB 40
BIT 0,C	CB 41
BIT 0,D	CB 42
BIT 0,E	CB 43
BIT 0,H	CB 44
BIT 0,L	CB 45
BIT 1,(HL)	CB 4E
BIT 1,(IX+dis)	DD CB XX 4E
BIT 1,(IY+dis)	FD CB XX 4E
BIT 1,A	CB 4F
BIT 1,B	CB 48
BIT 1,C	CB 49
BIT 1,D	CB 4A
BIT 1,E	CB 4B
BIT 1,H	CB 4C
BIT 1,L	CB 4D
BIT 2,(HL)	CB 56
BIT 2,(IX+dis)	DD CB XX 56
BIT 2,(IY+dis)	FD CB XX 56
BIT 2,A	CB 57

MNEMONIC	HEXADECIMAL
BIT 2,B	CB 50
BIT 2,C	CB 51
BIT 2,D	CB 52
BIT 2,E	CB 53
BIT 2,H	CB 54
BIT 2,L	CB 55
BIT 3,(HL)	CB 5E
BIT 3,(IX+dis)	DD CB XX 5E
BIT 3,(IY+dis)	FD CB XX 5E
BIT 3,A	CB 5F
BIT 3,B	CB 58
BIT 3,C	CB 59
BIT 3,D	CB 5A
BIT 3,E	CB 5B
BIT 3,H	CB 5C
BIT 3,L	CB 5D
BIT 4,(HL)	CB 66
BIT 4,(IX+dis)	DD CB XX 66
BIT 4,(IY+dis)	FD CB XX 66
BIT 4,A	CB 67
BIT 4,B	CB 60
BIT 4,C	CB 61
BIT 4,D	CB 62
BIT 4,E	CB 63
BIT 4,H	CB 64
BIT 4,L	CB 65
BIT 5,(HL)	CB 6E
BIT 5,(IX+dis)	DD CB XX 6E
BIT 5,(IY+dis)	FD CB XX 6E
BIT 5,A	CB 6F
BIT 5,B	CB 68
BIT 5,C	CB 69
BIT 5,D	CB 6A
BIT 5,E	CB 6B
BIT 5,H	CB 6C
BIT 5,L	CB 6D
BIT 6,(HL)	CB 76
BIT 6,(IX+dis)	DD CB XX 76
BIT 6,(IY+dis)	FD CB XX 76
BIT 6,A	CB 77
BIT 6,B	CB 70
BIT 6,C	CB 71
BIT 6,D	CB 72
BIT 6,E	CB 73
BIT 6,H	CB 74
BIT 6,L	CB 75
BIT 7,(HL)	CB 7E
BIT 7,(IX+dis)	DD CB XX 7E
BIT 7,(IY+dis)	FD CB XX 7E
BIT 7,A	CB 7F
BIT 7,B	CB 78
BIT 7,C	CB 79
BIT 7,D	CB 7A
BIT 7,E	CB 7B
BIT 7,H	CB 7C
BIT 7,L	CB 7D
CALL ADDR	CD XX XX
CALL C,ADDR	DC XX XX
CALL M,ADDR	FC XX XX
CALL NC,ADDR	D4 XX XX
CALL NZ,ADDR	C4 XX XX
CALL P,ADDR	F4 XX XX
CALL PE,ADDR	EC XX XX
CALL PO,ADDR	E4 XX XX
CALL Z,ADDR	CC XX XX
CCF	3F
CP (HL)	BE
CP (IX+dis)	DD BE XX
CP (IY+dis)	FD BE XX
CP A	BF
CP B	B8
CP C	B9
CP D	BA

MNEMONIC	HEXADECIMAL
CP n	FE XX
CP E	BB
CP H	BC
CP L	
CPD	
CPDR	
CPI	
CPIR	
CPL	
DAA	
DEC (HL)	35
DEC (IX+dis)	DD 35 XX
DEC (IY+dis)	FD 35 XX
DEC A	3D
DEC B	05
DEC BC	0B
DEC C	0D
DEC D	15
DEC DE	1B
DEC E	1D
DEC H	25
DEC HL	2B
DEC IX	DD 2B
DEC IY	FD 2B
DEC L	2D
DEC SP	3B
DI	F3
DJNZ,dis	10 XX
EI	FB
EX (SP) ,HL	E3
EX (SP) ,IX	DD E3
EX (SP) ,IY	FD E3
EX AF,AF'	08
EX DE,HL	EB
EXX	D9
HALT	76
IM 0	ED 46
IM 1	ED 56
IM 2	ED 5E
IN A, (C)	ED 78
IN A,port	DB XX
IN B, (C)	ED 40
IN C, (C)	ED 48
IN D, (C)	ED 50
IN E, (C)	ED 58
IN H, (C)	ED 60
IN L, (C)	ED 68
INC (HL)	34
INC (IX+dis)	DD 34 XX
INC (IY+dis)	FD 34 XX
INC A	3C
INC B	04
INC BC	03
INC C	0C
INC D	14
INC DE	13
INC E	1C
INC H	24
INC HL	23
INC IX	DD 23
INC IY	FD 23
INC L	2C
INC SP	33
IND	ED AA
INDR	ED BA
INI	ED A2
INIR	ED B2
JP (HL)	E9
JP (IX)	DD E9
JP (IY)	FD E9
JP ADDR	C3 XX XX
JP C,ADDR	DA XX XX
JP M,ADDR	FA XX XX

MNEMONIC	HEXADECIMAL
JP NC,ADDR	D2 XX XX
JP NZ,ADDR	C2 XX XX
JP P,ADDR	F2 XX XX
JP PE,ADDR	EA XX XX
JP PO,ADDR	E2 XX XX
JP Z,ADDR	CA XX XX
JR C,dis	38 XX
JR dis	18 XX
JR NC,dis	30 XX
JR NZ,dis	20 XX
JR Z,dis	28 XX
LD (ADDR) ,A	32 XX XX
LD(ADDR) ,BC	ED 43 XX XX
LD (ADDR) ,DE	ED 53 XX XX
LD(ADDR) ,HL	ED 63 XX XX
LD (ADDR) ,HL	22 XX XX
LD (ADDR) ,IX	DD 22 XX XX
LD (ADDR) , IY	FD 22 XX XX
LD (ADDR) ,SP	ED 73 XX XX
LD (BC) ,A	02
LD (DE) ,A	12
LD (HL) ,A	77
LD (HL) ,B	70
LD (HL), C	71
LD (HL) ,D	72
LD (HL) ,n	36 XX
LD (HL) ,E	73
LD (HL) ,H	74
LD (HL) ,L	75
LD (IX+dis) ,A	DD 77 XX
LD (IX+dis) ,B	DD 70 XX
LD (IX+dis) ,C	DD 71 XX
LD (IX+dis) ,D	DD 72 XX
LD (IX+dis) ,n	DD 36 XX XX
LD (IX+dis) ,E	DD 73 XX
LD (IX+dis) ,H	DD 74 XX
LD (IX+dis) ,L	DD 75 XX
LD (IY+dis) ,A	FD 77 XX
LD (IY+dis) ,B	FD 70 XX
LD (IY+dis) ,C	FD 71 XX
LD (IY+dis) ,D	FD 72 XX
LD (IY+dis) ,n	FD 36 XX XX
LD (IY+dis) ,E	FD 73 XX
LD (IY+dis) ,H	FD 74 XX
LD (IY+dis) ,L	FD 75 XX
LD A, (ADDR)	3A XX XX
LD A, (BC)	0A
LD A, (DE)	1A
LD A, (HL)	7E
LD A, (IX+dis)	DD 7E XX
LD A, (IY+dis)	FD 7E XX
LD A,A	7F
LD A,B	78
LD A,C	79
LD A,D	7A
LD A,n	3E XX
LD A,E	7B
LD A,H	7C
LD A,I	ED 57
LD A,L	7D
LD A,R	ED 5F
LD B, (HL)	46
LD B, (IX+dis)	DD 46 XX
LD B, (IY+dis)	FD 46 XX
LD B,A	47
LD B,B	40
LD B,C	41
LD B,D	42
LD B,n	06 XX
LD B,E	43
LD B,H	44
LD B,L	45
LD BC, (ADDR)	ED 4B XX XX

MNEMONIC	HEXADECIMAL
LD BC,nn	01 XX XX
LD C, (HL)	4E
LD C, (IX+dis)	DD 4E xx
LD C, (IY+dis)	FD 4E XX
LD C,A	4F
LD C,B	48
LD C,C	49
LD C,D	4A
LD C,n	0E XX
LD C,E	4B
LD C,H	4C
LD C,L	4D
LD D, (HL)	56
LD D, (IX+dis)	DD 56 XX
LD D, (IY+dis)	FD 56 XX
LD D,A	57
LD D,B	50
LD D,C	51
LD D,D	52
LD D,n	16 XX
LD D,E	53
LD D,H	54
LD D,L	55
LD DE, (ADDR)	ED 5B XX XX
LD DE,nn	11 XX XX
LD E, (HL)	5E
LD E, (IX+dis)	DD 5E XX
LD E, (IY+dis)	FD 5E XX
LD E,A	5F
LD E,B	58
LD E,C	59
LD E,D	5A
LD E,n	1E XX
LD E,E	5B
LD E,H	5C
LD E,L	5D
LD H, (HL)	66
LD H, (IX+dis)	DD 66 XX
LD H, (IY+dis)	FD 66 XX
LD H,A	67
LD H,B	60
LD H,C	61
LD H,D	62
LD H,n	26 XX
LD H,E	63
LD H,H	64
LD H,L	65
LD HL, (ADDR)	ED 6B XX XX
LD HL,(ADDR)	2A XX XX
LD HL,nn	21 XX XX
LD I,A	ED 47
LD IX, (ADDR)	DD 2A XX XX
LD IX,nn	DD 21 XX XX
LD IY (ADDR)	FD 2A XX XX
LD IY,nn	FD 21 XX XX
LD L,A	6F
LD L,B	68
LD L,C	69
LD L,D	6A
LD L,n	2E XX
LD L,E	6B
LD L, (HL)	6E
LD L,(IX+dis)	DD 6E XX
LD L, (IY+dis)	FD 6E XX
LD L,H	6C
LD L,L	6D
LD R,A	ED 4F
LD SP, (ADDR)	ED 7B XX XX
LD SP,nn	31 XX XX
LD SP,HL	F9
LD SP,IX	DD F9
LD SP,IY	FD F9
LDD	ED A8

MNEMONIC	HEXADECIMAL
LDDR	ED B8
LDI	ED A0
LDIR	ED B0
NEG	ED 44
NOP	00
OR (HL)	B6
OR (IX+dis)	DD B6 XX
OR (IY+dis)	FD B6 xx
OR A	B7
OR B	B0
OR C	B1
OR D	B2
OR n	F6 XX
OR E	B3
OR H	B4
OR L	B5
OTDR	ED BB
OTIR	ED B3
OUT (C) ,A	ED 79
OUT (C) ,B	ED 41
OUT (C) ,C	ED 49
OUT (C) ,D	ED 51
OUT (C) ,E	ED 59
OUT (C) ,H	ED 61
OUT (C) ,L	ED 69
OUT port,A	D3 port
OUTD	ED AB
OUTI	ED A3
POP AF	F1
POP BC	C1
POP DE	D1
POP HL	E1
POP IX	DD E1
POP IY	FD E1
PUSH AF	F5
PUSH BC	C5
PUSH DE	D5
PUSH HL	E5
PUSH IX	DD E5
PUSH IY	FD E5
RES 0, (HL)	CB 86
RES 0, (IX+dis)	DD CB XX 86
RES 0, (IY+dis)	FD CB XX 86
RES 0,A	CB 87
RES 0,B	CB 80
RES 0,C	CB 81
RES 0,D	CB 82
RES 0,E	CB 83
RES 0,H	CB 84
RES 0,L	CB 85
RES 1, (HL)	CB 8E
RES 1, (IX+dis)	DD CB XX 8E
RES 1, (IY+dis)	FD CB XX 8E
RES 1,A	CB 8F
RES 1,B	CB 88
RES 1,C	CB 89
RES 1,D	CB 8A
RES 1,E	CB 8B
RES 1,H	CB 8C
RES 1,L	CB 8D
RES 2, (HL)	CB 96
RES 2, (IX+dis)	DD CB XX 96
RES 2, (IY+dis)	FD CB XX 96
RES 2,A	CB 97
RES 2,B	CB 90
RES 2,C	CB 91
RES 2,D	CB 92
RES 2,E	CB 93
RES 2,H	CB 94
RES 2,L	CB 95
RES 3, (HL)	CB 9E
RES 3, (IX+dis)	DD CB XX 9E
RES 3, (IY+dis)	FD CB XX 9E
RES 3,A	CB 9F

MNEMONIC	HEXADECIMAL
RES 3,B	CB 98
RES 3,C	CB 99
RES 3,D	CB 9A
RES 3,E	CB 9B
RES 3,H	CB 9C
RES 3,L	CB 9D
RES 4, (HL)	CB A6
RES 4, (IX+dis)	DD CB XX A6
RES 4, (IY+dis)	FD CB XX A6
RES 4,A	CB A7
RES 4,B	CB A0
RES 4,C	CB A1
RES 4,D	CB A2
RES 4,E	CB A3
RES 4,H	CB A4
RES 4,L	CB A5
RES 5 (HL)	CB AE
RES 5, (IX+dis)	DD CB XX AE
RES 5, (IY+dis)	FD CB XX AE
RES 5,A	CB AF
RES 5,B	CB A8
RES 5,C	CB A9
RES 5,D	CB AA
RES 5,E	CB AB
RES 5,H	CB AC
RES 5,L	CB AD
RES 6, (HL)	CB B6
RES 6, (IX+dis)	DD CB XX B6
RES 6, (IY+dis)	FD CB XX B6
RES 6,A	CB B7
RES 6,B	CB B0
RES 6,C	CB B1
RES 6,D	CB B2
RES 6,E	CB B3
RES 6,H	CB B4
RES 6,L	CB B5
RES 7, (HL)	CB BE
RES 7, (IX+dis)	DD CB XX BE
RES 7, (IY+dis)	FD CB XX BE
RES 7,A	CB BF
RES 7,B	CB B8
RES 7,C	CB B9
RES 7,D	CB BA
RES 7,E	CB BB
RES 7,H	CB BC
RES 7,L	CB BD
RET	C9
RET C	D8
RET M	F8
RET NC	D0
RET NZ	C0
RET P	F0
RET PE	E8
RET PO	E0
RET Z	C8
RETI	ED 4D
RETN	ED 45
RL (HL)	CB 16
RL (IX+dis)	DD CB XX 16
RL (IY+dis)	FD CB XX 16
RL A	CB 17
RL B	CB 10
RL C	CB 11
RL D	CB 12
RL E	CB 13
RL H	CB 14
RL L	CB 15
RLA	17
RLC (HL)	CB 06
RLC (IX+dis)	DD CB XX 06
RLC (IY+dis)	FD CB XX 06
RLC A	CB 07
RLC B	CB 00

MNEMONIC	HEXADECIMAL
RLC C	CB 01
RLC D	CB 02
RLC E	CB 03
RLC H	CB 04
RLC L	CB 05
RLCA	07
RLD	ED 6F
RR (HL)	CB 1E
RR (IX+dis)	DD CB XX 1E
RR (IY+dis)	FD CB XX 1E
RR A	CB 1F
RR B	CB 18
RR C	CB 19
RR D	CB 1A
RR E	CB 1B
RR H	CB 1C
RR L	CB 1D
RRA	1F
RRC (HL)	CB 0E
RRC (IX+dis)	DD CB XX 0E
RRC (IY+dis)	FD CB XX 0E
RRC A	CB 0F
RRC B	CB 08
RRC C	CB 09
RRC D	CB 0A
RRC E	CH 0B
RRC H	CB 0C
RRC L	CB 0D
RRCA	0F
RRD	ED 67
RST 00	C7
RST 08	CF
RST 10	D7
RST 18	DF
RST 20	E7
RST 28	EF
RST 30	F7
RST 38	FF
SBC A, (HL)	9E
SBC A, (IX+dis)	DD 9E XX
SBC A, (IY+dis)	FD 9E XX
SBC A,A	9F
SBC A,B	98
SBC A,C	99
SBC A,D	9A
SBC A,n	DE XX
SBC A,E	9B
SBC A,H	9C
SBC A,L	9D
SBC HL,BC	ED 42
SBC HL,DE	ED 52
SBC HL,HL	ED 62
SBC HL,SP	ED 72
SCF	37
SET 0, (HL)	CB C6
SET 0, (IX+dis)	DD CB XX C6
SET 0, (IY+dis)	FD CB XX C6
SET 0,A	CB C7
SET 0,B	CB C0
SET 0,C	CB C1
SET 0,D	CB C2
SET 0,E	CB C3
SET 0,H	CB C4
SET 0,L	CB C5
SET 1, (HL)	CB CE
SET 1, (IX+dis)	DD CB XX CE
SET 1, (IY+dis)	FD CB XX CE
SET 1,A	CB CF
SET 1,B	CB C8
SET 1,C	CB C9
SET 1,D	CB CA
SET 1,E	CB CB
SET 1,H	CB CC

MNEMONIC	HEXADECIMAL
SET 1,L	CB CD
SET 2, (HL)	CB D6
SET 2, (IX+dis)	DD CB XX D6
SET 2, (IY+dis)	FD CB XX D6
SET 2,A	CB D7
SET 2,B	CB D0
SET 2,C	CB D1
SET 2,D	CB D2
SET 2,E	CB D3
SET 2,H	CB D4
SET 2,L	CB D5
SET 3, (HL)	CB DE
SET 3, (IX+dis)	DD CB XX DE
SET 3, (IY+dis)	FD CB XX DE
SET 3,A	CB DF
SET 3,B	CB D8
SET 3,C	CB D9
SET 3,D	CB DA
SET 3,E	CB DB
SET 3,H	CB DC
SET 3,L	CB DD
SET 4, (HL)	CBE6
SET 4, (IX+dis)	DD CB XX E6
SET 4, (IY+dis)	FD CB XX E6
SET 4,A	CB E7
SET 4,B	CB E0
SET 4,C	CB E1
SET 4,D	CB E2
SET 4,E	CB E3
SET 4,H	CB E4
SET 4,L	CB E5
SET 5, (HL)	CB EE
SET 5, (IX+dis)	DD CB XX EE
SET 5, (IY+dis)	FD CB XX EE
SET 5,A	CB EF
SET 5,B	CB E8
SET 5,C	CB E9
SET 5,D	CB EA
SET 5,E	CB EB
SET 5,H	CB EC
SET 5,L	CB ED
SET 6, (HL)	CB F6
SET 6, (IX+dis)	DD CB XX F6
SET 6, (IY+dis)	FD CB XX F6
SET 6,A	CB F7
SET 6,B	CB F0
SET 6,C	CB F1
SET 6,D	CB F2
SET 6,E	CB F3
SET 6,H	CB F4
SET 6,L	CB F5
SET 7, (HL)	CB FE
SET 7, (IX+dis)	DD CB XX FE
SET 7,(IY+dis)	FD CB XX FE
SET 7,A	CB FF
SET 7,B	CB F8
SET 7,C	CB F9
SET 7,D	CB FA
SET 7,E	CB FB
SET 7,H	CB FC
SET 7,L	CB FD
SLA (HL)	CB 26
SLA (IX+dis)	DD CB XX 26
SLA (IY+dis)	FD CB XX 26
SLA A	CB 27
SLA B	CB 20
SLA C	CB 21
SLA D	CB 22
SLA E	CB 23
SLA H	CB 24
SLA L	CB 25
SRA (HL)	CB 2E
SRA (IX+dis)	DD CB XX 2E

MNEMONIC	HEXADECIMAL	MNEMONIC	HEXADECIMAL	MNEMONIC	HEXADECIMAL
SRA (IY+dis)	FD CB XX 2E				
SRA A	CB 2F				
SRA B	CB 28				
SRA C	CB 29				
SRA D	CB 2A				
SRA E	CB 2B				
SRA H	CB 2C				
SRA L	CB 2D				
SRL (HL)	CB 3E				
SRL (IX+dis)	DD CB XX 3E				
SRL (IY+dis)	FD CB XX 3E				
SRL A	CB 3F				
SRL B	CB 38				
SRL C	CB 39				
SRL D	CB 3A				
SRL E	CB 3B				
SRL H	CB 3C				
SRL L	CB 3D				
SUB (HL)	96				
SUB (IX+dis)	DD 96 XX				
SUB (IY+dis)	FD 96 XX				
SUB A	97				
SUB B	90				
SUB C	91				
SUB D	92				
SUB E	D6 XX				
SUB n	93				
SUB H	94				
SUB L	95				
XOR (HL)	AE				
XOR (IX+dis)	DD AE XX				
XOR (IY+dis)	FD AE XX				
XOR A	AF				
XOR B	A9				
XOR C	A9				
XOR D	AA				
XOR n	EE XX				
XOR E	AB				
XSOR H	AC				
XOR L	AD				

Also Available

Made in the USA
Monee, IL
12 November 2026

cd37b099-62ce-4154-8686-73b3220cafc6R01

Made in the USA
Monee, IL
12 November 2026

cd37b099-62ce-4154-8686-73b3220cafc6R01